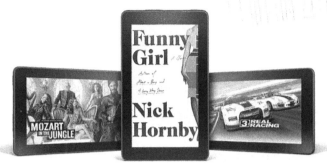

Fire Tablet Tips, Tricks, and Traps:

A guide to the new under $50 fire tablet

Edward C Jones

Fire Tablet Tips, Tricks, and Traps

© 30 September 2015 by Jones-Mack Technology Services of Charlotte, NC.

Digital rights provided by agreement to Amazon Digital Services, Inc.

Print edition rights provided by agreement to CreateSpace, an Amazon company

Amazon, Kindle, Fire, the Amazon logo, the Amazon Kindle logo

and the Fire logo are trademarks of Amazon.com, Inc. or its

affiliates.

INTRODUCTION

If you are the proud owner of the new Fire tablet, released by Amazon at an incredible price of just under $50 US, you're at the right place to learn all of what you need to know to use your Fire like a seasoned pro. In this comprehensive guide, you'll learn tips (ways to effectively use your Fire), tricks (ways to improve the operation of your Fire), and traps (things to avoid to prevent problems while using your Fire). You will learn-

- How to get around to the user interface, the home screen, and the carousel more efficiently
- How to make your Fire your own, customizing its display and operation for fastest and easiest use
- How to find THOUSANDS of FREE as in, 'zero dollars and zero cents') books
- How to use the built-in cameras to take photos and videos
- How to setup the security options to protect your account information
- How you can move your iTunes or other music library to your Fire
- How you can download YouTube videos to your Fire
- Suggested apps that no Fire owner should be without

You will learn all of the above and more, with *Fire Tablet Tips, Tricks, and Traps: A guide to the new under-$50 Fire tablet* as a part of your library. Read on, and learn 100% of what you need to know to get the most out of your Fire!

IMPORTANT NOTE: This book has been written EXCLUSIVELY for the Fire tablet, introduced in September 2015 and sold (at the time of its release) for just under $50 (USD). If you are using any other model of Fire tablet, see our *sister publications. For additional information go to the Amazon site, and search on the term 'Edward Jones kindle fire.'*

Table of Contents

INTRODUCTION 5
Chapter 1: Fire Out of the Box 11
About the Fire 12
Which model of Fire do I own? 12
About tablet computers 13
About Your Tablet 13
Where's My Data? (Your Fire Storage, and the Amazon
Cloud) 15
History of the Fire 18
Setting up your Fire 20
Controls and Layout of the Fire tablet 21
Chapter 2: User-Interface Tips, Tricks, and Traps 25
About the Home Screen, Navigation Bar, App Grid, and
Favorites 25
Using the Task Switcher 29
Setting your Display 30
Customizing your Favorites 32
Changing Basic Settings on your Fire 32
General Typing and Text-Entry Tips 38
Using the Swype keyboard feature 40
Chapter 3: Getting Content (TV, movies, books, and music) 43
Buying books, magazines, and periodicals 45
Buying or renting movies or TV shows 46
Buying and downloading music from Amazon's Music
Store 47
Removing content from your device 49
Getting Kindle Books from your local library (without
setting foot in your library) 49
Using the Kindle Owner's Lending Library ("KOLL") to
your advantage 51
Easily Search the Kindle Store for Free Books 51
Chapter 4: Silk browser tips, tricks, and traps 55
Surfing the Web with the Silk Browser 55
Using Bookmarks 57
Changing Silk Settings for Best Operation 58

Chapter 5: File Management Tips, Tricks and Traps 61
Sending Files to your Fire via E-mail 62
Transferring Files to your Fire with its Charging Cable.... 65
Transferring Files Wirelessly with the Wi-Fi File Explorer
App 66
Adding file storage space with a Micro SD Ram Card 67
Chapter 6: Email Tips, Tricks, and Traps........................... 71
Setting up your Fire E-mail 71
Setting up E-mail manually 75
Reading your E-Mail 77
Switching between multiple mail accounts 79
Composing and Sending Mail 79
Customize your E-mail operation with various settings.... 82
Using your synchronized calendars and contacts 84
Chapter 7: Multimedia Tips, Tricks, and Traps.................. 89
Playing personal videos on your Fire 89
Importing your Music Library from other sources to your
Fire 91
Downloading and playing YouTube videos 92
Storing pictures and personal videos in the Amazon
CloudDrive 93
Viewing your CloudDrive photos on a Fire 95
Chapter 8: Camera Tips, Trips, and Traps......................... 97
Using the Fire's built-in Camera app............................... 98
Viewing photos with the Camera Roll.............................. 99
Editing and Deleting Photos 100
Sharing your photos with others 102
An important note about photo & video storage and the
Amazon Cloud Drive.. 102
Getting photos from your Fire onto your computer......... 103
Adding capabilities with third-party camera apps........... 104
General Camera tips 104
Chapter 9: Apps Tips, Tricks, and Traps........................... 107
About Apps.. 107
Deleting Apps 109
Troubleshooting Apps 110
Twelve FREE Apps That No Fire Should Be Without.... 112
Crackle... 114

Netflix 115
IMDb.. 116
USA Today 117
ESPN ScoreCenter 119
Facebook by Facebook 120
Calculator Plus FREE by Digital Cherry, LLC 121
Kayak 122
CruiseFinder.. 123
YP Local Search and Gas Prices (Kindle tablet edition) . 124
iTranslate by Sonico Mobile........................... 125
Chapter 10: Printing from your Fire 129
Printing using Google's Cloud Print Services 130
Chapter 11: Security Tips, Tricks, and Traps 135
Chapter 12: Battery and Power Tips, Tricks, and Traps...... 139
CONCLUSION (and a favor to ask!) 143

Chapter 1: Fire Out of the Box

Welcome to *Fire Tablet Tips, Tricks, and Traps: A guide to the all-new Fire*. This is a user's guide, written to get beginners up to speed quickly, as well as to provide content that will also appeal to the more technically-savvy. In this book, you will find all the basic tips you need to quickly learn to use your Fire like a seasoned pro. And the more advanced topics covered in this book will help you take your use of the Fire to a higher level, getting the most out of your new tablet.

This book looks at three categories in every chapter: *tips*, *tricks*, and *traps*.

Tips are techniques that make things easier in terms of use, in a particular area.

Tricks are techniques that change the operation of your Fire in a particular area, often providing capabilities or performance improvements that just were not there out of the box.

Traps are "gotchas," things to watch out for, that can cause problems.

About the Fire

The Fire is one product in a line of products known as Amazon Fire tablets. Fire tablets are handheld devices, designed and sold by Amazon that let you view movies and TV shows, download music, and shop for and download e-books, magazines, and other digital content using wireless technology. At the time of this writing, Fire tablets are available in four different models: the Fire with a 7-inch screen, the Fire HD6 with a 6-inch screen, the Fire HD8 with an 8-inch screen, and the Fire HD10 with a 10-inch (diagonal measurement) screen.

Which model of Fire do I own?

If you received your Fire tablet as a gift and you're uncertain as to which model you possess, a simple way to tell is to diagonally measure the screen. The Fire measures 7 inches diagonally while the Fire HD8 measures roughly 8 inches diagonally, and the Fire HD10 measures slightly over 10 inches in length. The Fire tablet is also somewhat thicker than the HD8 and HD10 models, with the Fire tablet measuring 0.4 inches when compared to the HD8 and HD10 which are both 0.3 inches in thickness.

About tablet computers

The Fire falls squarely within the market of handheld computers generally referred to as tablets, and tablets occupy the market space between smartphones and laptop computers. Tablets generally possess all or nearly all the functions of laptop computers, two notable exceptions being that tablets generally lack physical keyboards and have smaller screens. An appealing feature of tablet computers is that, like smartphones, they can run "apps." Apps, short for applications, are small computer programs that run within the tablet's internal memory and literally re-define the operation of the tablet. Apps can give your Fire the ability to act as far more than an e-book reader or a movie player. You can download and install apps that transform your Fire into a digital butler, an electronic medical advisor, a powerful financial analyst, or a first-rate game platform.

Within the tablet marketplace, the Fire compares favorably to other low-cost ($300 US and under) devices that typically sport 7-inch screens and run apps designed either for the Android operating system or for Apple's iOS operating system. Devices currently in this marketplace include the Apple iPad Mini line, Google's Nexus, and the Samsung Galaxy Tab line as well as Amazon's own Fire HD8 and HD10.

About Your Tablet

Your Fire tablet is, in the opinion of the author, a remarkable value for the price. The Fire tablet costs just under $50 (U.S.) or just under £50 (U.K.), and Amazon offers a "buy five, get one free" deal which translates to just under $42 per tablet, if you have this number of family or friends on your shopping list. In return for the funds spent, you get a tablet with a 7-inch color LCD screen (measured diagonally) that can be used for watching movies and TV, reading books, listening to music, running thousands of apps, and more.

Fire tablet (photo courtesy Amazon, Inc.)

The screen resolution of a Fire tablet is rated at 1024 by 600 pixels, and the device is powered by a 1.3 GHZ quad-core processor with 8 GB of memory (expandable to 128 GB with the addition of an optional micro SD Ram card). Two cameras, a built-in microphone, headphone jack and a built-in mono speaker round out the package.

And while there have been various android tablets at the $50 price point from big box retailers in the past, such tablets have suffered from inconsistent quality and a lack of features (such as offering a single camera or slow response due to the lack of a quad-core processor). By comparison, the Fire tablet provides a full set of features in a package that's responsive and well-built. The following table shows the specifications for the Fire tablet.

Screen Size	7"
Resolution	1024 x 600 (171 ppi)
Processor	Quad-core 1.3 GHz
Audio	Mono speaker, built-in microphone
Storage	8 GB (expandable by up to 128 GB), with free unlimited cloud storage for Amazon content
Cameras	VGA Front-facing camera and 2 MP rear-facing camera with 720p HD video recording

Connectivity	Single-band Wi-Fi supporting b/g/n bands
Battery Life	7 hours
Size	7.5" x 4.5" x 0.4"
Weight	11.0 oz (313 g)

Fire tablet specifications

Where's My Data? (Your Fire Storage, and the Amazon Cloud)

With the popularity of tablets, you may have heard talk of what may be a somewhat magical and mystical place known as "the cloud." Your Fire has 8 gigabytes of built-in data storage along with a slot for the addition of a micro SD RAM card, allowing the internal storage to be expanded by up to 128 gigabytes of storage.

This may sound like a lot of space, but in the grand scheme of things, it really is not. (By comparison, the average personal computer sold at the time of this writing typically has a hard drive measuring around a terabyte (1,000 gigabytes) in size, and a single Blu-Ray DVD movie occupies roughly 25 gigabytes.) If you tried to store large amounts of digital content- especially movies and videos- on your Fire, you would quickly exhaust its usable space. To get around this problem, the Fire (and many other tablets) store large amounts of information in the cloud, which is another name for data servers that are accessed from the Internet. Amazon's servers are referred to as the Amazon Cloud, and all Fire owners have access to unlimited amounts of data storage for their purchases in the Amazon Cloud. The portion of the Amazon Cloud that's assigned to your Amazon account is called the Amazon Cloud Drive.

Content that you purchase from Amazon is stored in either of two places: in your cloud storage on Amazon's servers, and on your Fire itself. (Often, your content is stored in two places simultaneously: when you download an item, it is stored both on your device, and a copy of it remains in the

Amazon cloud.) When you initially purchase a book, a song, a game, or an app (even free content is purchased, you just aren't charged for this), the content is initially stored in your personal space in the Amazon Cloud, where the content is not taking up any space on your Fire. When you press the Download button that appears on the icon for that content in the cloud, it gets downloaded to the memory space of your Fire itself.

If you display a given category on your Fire, such as apps, books, or music, at the top center of the screen you will see icons for *Library* and *Store*, as shown in the illustration that follows.

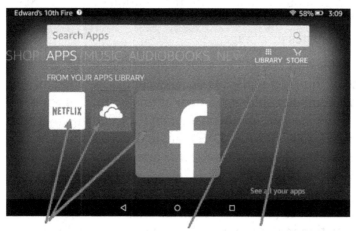

Apps stored on your Fire

Library shows apps stored in the Amazon Cloud

Store shows apps available through the Amazon AppStore

By default, the content that is stored on your Fire appears on the screen. You can tap Library to see all of the content that is stored on Amazon's cloud under your account. You can download content from the cloud onto your device anytime you have an active Wi-Fi connection, and you can delete content from the device as necessary to ensure that you have plenty of room for new content.

If you are curious as to whether you are running short of storage space on your device, you can quickly determine your available remaining storage space. Get to the Home screen, swipe down from the top of the screen, and tap Settings. At the Settings screen that appears, in the Device area, tap Storage. Your Fire will display a Storage screen, similar to the example shown in the following illustration. (In the illustration, colors have been reversed from the Fire's actual screen display to improve readability.)

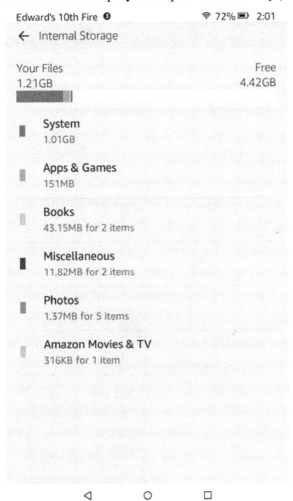

The Storage screen tells you how much space is available, and how much space is currently being used by various categories, such as books and newsstand items, audio books, music, videos, and photos.

History of the Fire

This portion of this chapter certainly isn't required reading if you are to become an accomplished user of your Fire, but it is a fascinating success story. The Fire is one of a line of products that all sprang from the original Amazon Kindle, a revolutionary device inspired by a revolutionary individual, Amazon founder and CEO Jeff Bezos. During the nascent days of the World Wide Web, it was Bezos who came up with the idea of selling books online, rather than in the traditional bricks and mortar bookstore environment, and Bezos founded Amazon, billed as the world's largest bookstore. Books were very good to Bezos and to Amazon, catapulting the company to a multibillion dollar global enterprise and taking Bezos to billionaire status in the process. But even though Bezos himself was (and is, according to reports) an avid book reader, he recognized something: a cornerstone of Amazon's long-term future in the 21st century, the printed book, was a likely candidate for obsolescence by the end of the 21st century, if not sooner. Music had gone digital, video was in the process of moving in that direction, and for the printed book, the same transition was simply a matter of time. Having built a better bookstore, Bezos believed he could improve upon one of humanity's greatest inventions- the printed book- by taking it digital.

In 2004, Bezos turned a group of engineers loose in an Amazon subsidiary, Lab126, based in Cupertino, California, and charged them with the task of developing a digital replacement for the printed book. Roughly three years later, in November of 2007, Amazon placed the fruits of Bezos dream and the engineers' labors- the original Amazon Kindle- on sale. It used a patented E-ink display that was capable of rendering 16 shades to simulate reading on paper while using minimal amounts of power. Content for the Amazon Kindle could be purchased online and downloaded wirelessly. (The name "Kindle" was the brainchild of consultants hired by the Lab126 division of Amazon, who felt that like kindling, it had the potential to light a fire- and that is exactly what the device began to do in the book publishing world.)

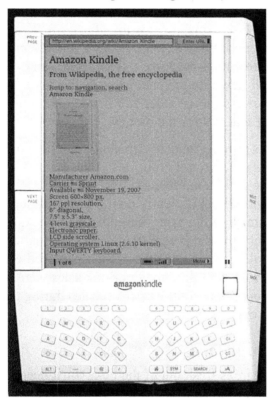

First Amazon Kindle (photo credit: Wikipedia)

Despite the fact that the device cost nearly $400 US, Amazon sold out its initial manufacturing run in a little over five and one half hours, and the Kindle remained out of stock until late April of 2008. The success of the original Amazon Kindle led to a family of devices, and as technology continued to advance and manufacturing costs continued to drop, the Fire became a product in Amazon's Kindle family. Announced in September of 2011, the original Fire was

Amazon's first Kindle to sport a liquid crystal display-based color screen, rather than the patented black on white E-ink display used by all the earlier Kindles. The Fire not only included access to Amazon's AppStore, but could also display streaming movies and TV shows as well as run 'apps,' in addition to being used to read books. (For a number of years since the Fire's first product launch, the product was referred to as the Kindle Fire. Amazon now uses the term "Kindle" to refer to its e-ink based line of book readers, and refers to the color LCD-based tablets as "Fire," "Fire HD8," and "Fire HD10.") The all-new Fire tablet covered in this book has been praised by reviewers for its under $50 price point, with an extensive set of features for the money.

Since its product launch, Amazon's Fire line of tablets has been a clear success, with millions of the devices sold. And while there's still a number of years left to this 21st century, the handwriting is clearly on the wall with regards to the eventual demise of the paper-based book. The Association of American Publishers reported that in the first quarter of 2012, e-book sales surpassed those of their paper-based counterparts for the first time- adult eBook sales were reported at $282.3 million, while adult hardcover sales during that same period reached only $229.6 million.

Setting up your Fire

If your Fire is fresh out of the box, you'll need to power up your new tablet and you'll need to set it up before you can begin using it. Before you start, make sure you have your Amazon username and password, and you will also need to be within range of an active Wi-Fi connection.

When you first turn your Fire on, you'll be asked to choose your language. (At the screen that asks you to select a language you can also change the default display text size by tapping a size shown at the lower left corner.) Make your desired selection and tap Continue, and at the next screen you'll select a Wi-Fi network and enter a password (if yours is a secured network). After entering your Wi-Fi network information, your Fire will connect to your network and may download a system update if necessary.

The next screen that appears will ask you for registration information. If you purchased your Fire tablet directly from Amazon while logged in with your Amazon account, your tablet will have been pre-registered for you. If not, you'll need to register your Fire. Enter your Amazon account details, or, if you don't have an Amazon account, choose Create an account and follow the instructions that appear on the screen.

Next, you'll get to choose your time zone, and confirm your account information. Make your selections and tap Continue, and you will see options for automatically backing up your Fire, for saving your Wi-Fi information, and for automatically saving photos and videos to the Amazon Cloud. Make your selections and tap Continue.

You will also be given the option to set up your Facebook and/or Twitter accounts. (You can do this now, or skip this step and save this for later.)

Finally, you will see some on-screen hints and tips that will help you get started with your Fire. If you already have Amazon Fire or Amazon Kindle content linked to your device, or apps from the Amazon App Store, they will all be available for download from the Amazon Cloud (more on this topic shortly). Your recently-read Kindle books will appear in an area known as the App Grid automatically, along with the latest apps and other downloaded content.

Controls and Layout of the Fire tablet

Take the time to get familiar with the physical aspects of your Fire. The following illustration shows the layout of various components. Along the upper edge of your Fire tablet, you'll find the power button, a Micro

USB port (used for recharging your Fire or for connecting your Fire to a computer), a built-in microphone, two buttons used to adjust the volume, and a headphone jack. At the upper right side, you'll find a cover for an expansion slot used to add optional memory storage in the form of a Micro SD RAM card.

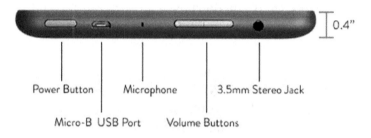

Power Button   Microphone   3.5mm Stereo Jack

Micro-B USB Port   Volume Buttons

Get familiar with the various parts of the Fire's user interface. The next chapter will detail this area extensively, but out of the box, it helps to know about the areas that you will be working with on your Fire screen. The following illustration shows these areas.

Device Name   Wi-Fi indicator   Battery level   Current time

Menu bar

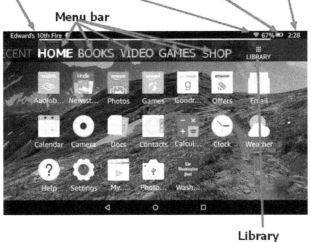

Library
(access to
Amazon Cloud)

You can get quick access to items that you use regularly by placing them in a desired area of that particular category. (You can view all of your content within a given category by swiping the entire screen upwards with one finger.)

To install any saved apps, in the Menu Bar tap on Apps, then tap on the Library icon. Tap on any of the icons to start that particular app downloading onto your device.

You can import your iTunes or similar music collection from your computer to your Fire. To import an existing music collection, you'll have to set up the Amazon Cloud Player on your tablet. Open a browser window on your computer, and visit amazon.com/cloudplayer (if you are in North America) or visit amazon.co.uk/cloudplayer (if you are in the United Kingdom) to begin importing the music from your computer into Cloud Player, which can then be streamed or downloaded onto your Fire.

Having problems??? When in doubt, reboot. Your Fire is a sophisticated computer, and like all computers, it may hiccup for unexplainable reasons at times. If your Fire freezes or locks up and refuses to respond to any actions, perform a hard reset. (You needn't worry about losing any memory settings with this type of reset; it just halts any programs currently running and shuts down your device.) Hold the power button depressed for at least 20 seconds and then release the button. Wait another 10 seconds, then turn on your Fire.

If you are experiencing an unusually high number of system lock-ups, make sure your battery charge level is not very low. A nearly fully-drained battery is a common cause of random Fire freezes.

Chapter 2: User-Interface Tips, Tricks, and Traps

The ***user interface*** (that's techno-speak for "the way you get along with the device") is fairly intuitive on a Fire, and that is by design. Amazon engineers have done a credible job of making the tablet easy to use, and with a market dominated by a product like Apple's iPad, that was an understandable goal. Nevertheless, there are things that you can do to make the way that you use your Fire more efficient, and that is what this chapter is all about.

About the Home Screen, Navigation Bar, App Grid, and Favorites

The Fire is based on a heavily modified version of Google's Android operating system. For the technically minded among readers, the first generation Fire was based on the Honeycomb version of the Android operating system, and upgrades to later models in existence resulted in the last shipments of first-gen units based on the Ice Cream Sandwich version of the Android operating system. Successive generations of Fire tablets used customized versions of the Jelly Bean and KitKat versions of the Android OS. The Fire tablet runs Fire OS 5 "Bellini," which is a heavily-customized version of the "Lollipop" variation of the Android operating system.

In any case, all Fires make use of a user interface that is very different than that of a generic Android tablet. Power up a Fire and you won't see the desktop-like design of an Android tablet. Instead, you will see Amazon's own customized interface called the Home screen, shown in the next illustration. Pardon the intentional repetition, but the illustration, which was shown in the prior chapter, is displayed once more here. In this chapter, we go into more detail about the parts of the Fire user interface, and how you can best use these features.

Device Name   Wi-Fi indicator   Battery level   Current time

Menu bar

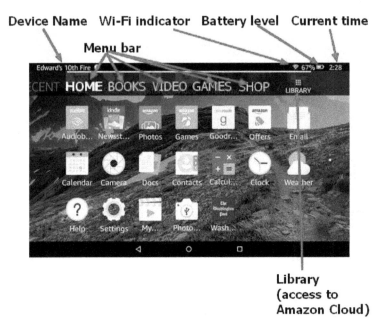

Library
(access to
Amazon Cloud)

(The Home screen of the Fire)

From the Home screen, your books, apps, music, and videos are all accessible with a swipe of the ***Menu Bar***. Simply swipe the Menu bar to the left or right and tap the desired category such as apps, games, books, music, or videos to display all of the items within that category. And there is a ***Search icon*** (in the shape of a magnifying glass) that can be used to search the entire device content, to search Amazon's massive library of content, or to just search the web.

The home screen can be divided into areas known as the App Grid (the area in the center of the screen), the menu bar at the top, and a Navigation Bar (at the bottom of the screen). From the Home screen, you can view any recently-accessed content by swiping from the left side of the screen, and you can swipe from the right side of the screen to view the dedicated content pages for your apps, books, movies, music, and more. (Note that the area now known as the *app grid* was referred to as the *Carousel* in previous versions of Fire tablets, so you may hear it referred to by that term in some publications.)

At the top of the home screen, the menu bar can be used to access any of your content pages. Just swipe the menu bar left or right and tap the desired category, such as Music or Books. Beneath the menu bar, your most recently-accessed content appears automatically. Tapping any content page displays both any recently accessed content for that category, as well as recommendations based on your past content tastes.

At the bottom of every screen, you'll find the Navigation Bar. (If you are in full-screen mode, you can always bring the Navigation Bar into view by either tapping on the center of the screen or by dragging down from the top of the screen.) Using the Navigation Bar, you can-

◁ Tap Back to return to any previous content you were using

○ Tap Home to go to your Home screen, or-

□ Tap Switch to open the Task Switcher, which you can use to open or close your recently-used apps.

Content pages are dedicated pages for books, video, games, and other content. Each page less you easily access recently opened or purchased items or browse the Amazon stores for new content. You can navigate between the different content pages by swiping left or right, or by tapping a desired page. And you can view your existing content or view new content recommendations by simply swiping upwards on a content page.

tip! **Understand the difference between the app grid and your *Library*.** The area in the center of the screen (called the app grid, or carousel in previous versions of Fire tablets) grows dynamically as you use your Fire, because an icon for everything that you've recently used on your Fire will appear within the App Grid and will remain for some time unless you delete it from the App Grid. With your Library, on the other hand, nothing appears automatically. You must add an item to the Library area in order for it to appear

You can get quick access to items that you use regularly by placing them on your Home screen. You can view all of your regularly-used content by swiping the entire screen upwards with one finger. To add a book, song, movie, game, or app to your Home screen, first use the Menu bar at the top of the screen. When a desired category appears, press and hold a desired item until a popup menu appears, then select Add to Home from the menu.

Clean up your Home screen. Over time, your Home screen can become overly cluttered with icons for all the items you've accessed on your Fire. To delete items from the Home screen, press and hold the unwanted item until a popup menu appears, and select Remove from Home from the menu.

Know how to come home. One of the first things any young child learns is how to come home, and any new Fire user should know how to get to the home screen as well. From anywhere you are at, drag down from the top of the screen or tap in the center of the screen, and the home icon will appear at the bottom center of the screen. Tap Home and you will return to the home screen.

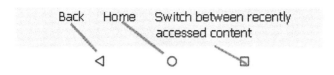

Back   Home   Switch between recently accessed content

◁   O   ▣

Check out the Amazon Help Video.

Amazon has taken the time to provide a short help video for this topic. At the Amazon web site, tap or click 'Help' (just below the Search box), and at the next page, under 'Browse Help Topics' select 'Amazon devices' and at the right, choose 'Fire HD8' or 'Fire HD10' as is appropriate. Under 'Fire tablet basics,' tap or click the 'Navigate Your Fire' link.

Using the Task Switcher

At any given point in time, you may have more than one app running in the background on your Fire. You can switch between apps at the touch of an icon using the Task Switcher. To access the Task Switcher, tap in the center of the screen until the Navigation Bar appears at the bottom of the screen, then tap the Task Switcher icon at the right side of the Navigation Bar. An example of the Task Switcher is shown in the following illustration:

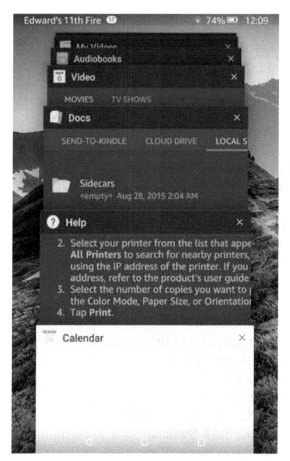

You can swipe upwards or downwards to reveal the individual pages for each app. Touch the icon for any desired app, and you will immediately switch to that app.

Setting your Display

Adjust your font sizes to make reading easiest on YOU. The Fire is a great multimedia device, but the entire Fire tablet line began life as an e-book reader, and millions of people still use it primarily for that purpose. You can easily adjust the font sizes to fit your needs. With any book open, tap in the center of the screen until a menu bar appears at the top of the screen, and then tap the Text (Aa) icon within the menu bar. You will see a dialog box like the one shown in the following illustration.

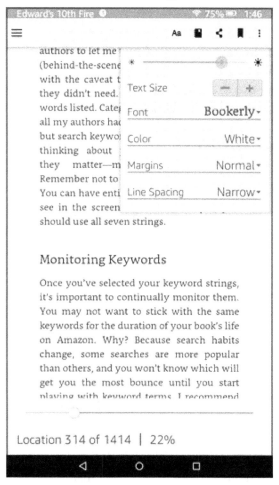

Tap the minus symbol under 'Text Size' to shrink the text, or tap the plus symbol under 'Text Size' to enlarge the text. You can also try the different Color Mode settings (white, sepia, and black) to see if you prefer one of these different backgrounds for your book reading. The lower rows within the dialog box contain options that let you adjust the margin width or the line spacing. And you can tap the Font name list box (displaying 'Bookerly' in this illustration) to display additional fonts that you can choose for your display.

Note that the Fire tablet display settings will control the text display of most e-books, but may not have an effect on some magazines. Many of the magazine publishers use their own settings menus to change the way the magazine is displayed.

Customizing your Favorites

You can rearrange the items within your content pages to suit your liking. Just long-press on an item, then slide your finger to a new location. The remaining items will automatically rearrange themselves.

Use 'Search' to find anything stored on your Kindle. While many Fire users think of the search field as a way to search for content such as books or movies, you can actually use the Search field to find any item that is stored on your device. Just go to the Home screen, tap the magnifying glass to bring up the Search field, and type a few letters. Search will bring up all items- books, videos, music, games, and so on- that match the letters you've typed. Tap anywhere above the keyboard to put the keyboard away, scroll to the desired item, and tap the item to open the item or launch an app.

Changing Basic Settings on your Fire

Using the Settings options of your Fire, you can change various settings that affect the behavior of your Fire.

You can modify Wi-Fi settings, display options, storage options, how your various apps behave, and more.

Amazon has taken the time to provide a short help video on the subject of settings for your Fire. CLICK HERE to go to the Fire Tablet Help Videos page, and when a video begins playing, scroll down and click the 'Settings' link.

Know your status. Swipe down from the top of your Fire, and a Quick Settings window will open showing various settings and other current information about your Fire, as shown in the following illustration.

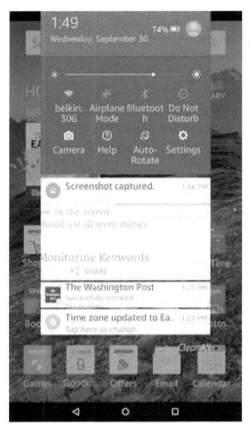

Auto-rotate: your Fire contains a gyroscope, which senses when the device is rotated, causing the display to shift between portrait and landscape mode. There are times when this is more of an annoyance than a help, such as when you are reading with the Kindle lying on a flat surface such as a tabletop. Tap the Auto-rotate icon to change the setting to locked, to disable the auto rotate function.

Brightness: Use the slider bar at the top of the window to increase or decrease screen brightness.

Wireless: Tapping the wireless option brings up another screen which lets you view or change your Wi-Fi network settings.

Airplane Mode and Bluetooth: You can use the Airplane Mode option to enable or disable Airplane Mode (turning off wireless transmission for when you are using your Fire in flight), and you can use the Bluetooth option to enable Bluetooth device settings (for sharing data with other Bluetooth-equipped devices such as many modern laptops, portable keyboards, and some smart phones.

Help: This icon, when pressed, displays a help screen that lets you get help with wireless connectivity issues, open the user guide for your Fire, or contact Amazon customer service, either via e-mail or by phone.

Settings: Tapping the settings icon will display a settings screen, as shown in the example that follows.

From here, you can access a variety of settings for your Fire, by simply tapping on the appropriate subcategory within the Settings screen. For example, you can tap the Display and Sounds subcategory to display a screen that lets you adjust the screen brightness display timeout (how long before your Fire tablet goes to sleep), and the behavior of the Fire when the device is rotated. You can tap the Security subcategory to create a locking password that prevents your Fire from being used by unauthorized users who do not know the password that you set for your device. You'll find many of these individual subcategories and their options explained in further detail in later parts of this book.

Of particular interest is the Device subcategory under the Settings screen. (To get here, drag down from the the top of the screen, and tap the Settings icon within the window that appears. In the Settings screen, tap Device to reveal the screen shown in the following illustration.) Here you can gain access to a number of settings that govern the individual behavior of your Fire.

The Device screen provides a visual indication of the state of your battery charge, the name of your device and its serial number. You can adjust your date and time settings, and even reset the device to its original factory settings (useful when it is time to upgrade to a more powerful Fire tablet, and pass on your trusted Fire to a close friend or relative).

General Typing and Text-Entry Tips

Make the keyboard larger. Most Fire apps work in portrait or landscape mode, and the keyboard is much larger and easier to use in landscape mode. Rotate the Fire 90 degrees to get a landscape view of the keyboard, for an easier typing experience.

When typing large amounts of text, end each sentence with a fast double-space. Heavy duty word processing on a Fire (or any similarly sized tablet) is going to be somewhat challenging due to the combination of a soft keyboard and small screen size. One time saving tip when doing a lot of typing on the Fire is at the end of each sentence, tap the spacebar quickly twice. A fast double-space will automatically insert a period, followed by a single space. You can then continue on to the next sentence.

The Fire really does have a Caps Lock key. For those times when you need to type a string of characters as ALL UPPERCASE LETTERS, the Fire does have the equivalent of a PC's Caps Lock key. Just double-tap the Shift key, and an orange bar will appear underneath the Shift symbol on the key indicator indicating that you are in Caps Lock mode. Type your upper case letters, then press the Shift key once more to drop out of Caps Lock mode.

Use the numbers shortcut to quickly enter numbers. If you are typing text, you don't need to switch between the letters keyboard and the numbers and symbols keyboard just to enter a number. The top row of letters can be long-pressed to enter a number. From left to right, a long-press on any of the top row of keys produce numbers from 1 through 9, followed by 0. Press and hold a top row letter until a number appears in orange, then release, to type that number.

Use the second and third row keyboard keys for most commonly used punctuation characters. If you closely examine the Fire's soft keyboard, you will see various non-alpha characters displayed at the upper right corner of each key. If you perform a long press on a particular key, the character shown in the upper-right corner of the key will appear, and you can release your finger to enter that character.

Your finger can serve as an insertion pointer. When editing large amounts of text, tap your finger on any empty area to display the Editing Tool. You can then press on it and move your fingertip within the text that you already typed, then release and edit the text as desired. When done editing, tap again at the end of the text, and continue typing.

Access the Cut-Copy-and-Paste options with a long-press on any word. If you need to cut or copy

39

and paste during text editing, long-press on any single word, and cut / copy / paste editing options will appear, along with two selection handles. Drag the selection handles to highlight the desired text, then long-press on the desired text, and choose Cut or Copy. To paste the cut or copied text elsewhere, just long press at the desired location, and tap Paste.

Using the Swype keyboard feature

All Fire tablets running the Fire 4.0 operating system or higher support an implementation of the popular 'swype' keyboard for touchscreens, and you need not perform any steps to activate the feature; it is enabled by default whenever the keyboard appears. With swype, you press and hold at the first letter of a word, then drag across to each successive letter in the word. As an example, if you wanted to type the name 'edward' you would press and hold the 'e' key, then drag to 'd' then 'w' then 'a' then 'r' and finally back to 'd', releasing touch at the final letter, as illustrated here. As you drag, an orange line shows the path of your last action.

The swipe feature has a level of artificial intelligence built in, so even if you miss a letter in a sequence, it will usually make the proper guess as to the intended word. Some users swear by it, while others don't care for the technique (I'm more of a voice dictation fan myself), but if you perform any amount of typing on your Fire, it's probably worth a try to see if the technique works for you.

Chapter 3: Getting Content (TV, movies, books, and music)

Your Fire is a great source of reading and entertainment, but let's face it: content costs, and quality contents costs more. Like everyone else, authors and songwriters certainly expect to eat (no surprise there), and production costs skyrocket when you get into the league of big-name entertainers and the costs of producing those Hollywood blockbusters that you're fond of watching on the 'small screen'. But there are great sources of free, quality content available for your Fire. In this chapter, we will first examine the wealth of content available from Amazon, and we will follow this with an examination of free content and where to find such content.

Amazon has integrated the Fire to provide a first class shopping experience through the Amazon stores. (The phrase 'stores', plural, is intentional, because with the company's growth, Amazon has divided their online retail store into a collection of stores.) You can think of it as having all of the convenience of a mall-- different stores, each specializing in carrying a broad assortment of products in a specific area-- with none of the disadvantages of a mall (noisy crowds, unruly teenagers, or bad food at the food court). Amazon has divided its digital stores into multiple categories, such as books and audiobooks, music, movies and TV, newsstand, apps and videogames, audiobooks, and Amazon Prime. At the Home

screen, tap Shop, then tap the Store icon at the upper-right, and open the menu by tapping the menu icon (the three horizontal bars at the upper left). You will see links for the different stores at the left side of the page that appears, as shown in the following illustration. Tap Departments, and the various store departments (books and audiobooks, movies and TV, music, and so on) will appear, and you can select and browse within or search a desired department.

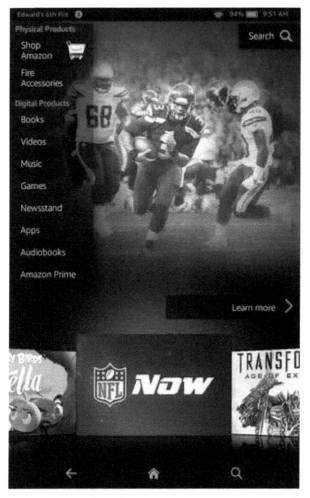

To make shopping easier, you will probably want to set up 1-Click ordering as a payment method. 1-Click ordering places your order automatically, letting you skip the hassle of a digital shopping cart. When you place your first order at Amazon and enter a payment method and shipping address, 1-Click ordering is enabled automatically. If you click Buy now with 1-Click on any product page, your order is automatically charged to the default payment method registered to your account, and it is shipped to the default address.

You can also use 1-click to ship to multiple shipping addresses. Perhaps you wish to have some items shipped to you at your job, others at your primary home, and some at your vacation home. Login to your Amazon account through a web browser, and click Manage Your Account. At the next screen, click Manage Addresses and 1-Click Settings. At the next screen that appears, you can enter more than one shipping address.

When you save multiple shipping addresses, and you order an item, a list box with all of your addresses will appear. You can then choose the desired address to have the item shipped to that location.

Note: You must have cookies enabled within your computers' web browser to use 1-Click shopping. ("Cookies" are small chunks of data stored by your browser which are used by Amazon, as well as by many online banks and stores, to identify your account.) If you have not enabled cookies within your browser, you can still purchase items by adding them to the Amazon Shopping Cart, and clicking Proceed to checkout when you are ready to complete your order.

Buying books, magazines, and periodicals

Once you've connected wirelessly and you've set up your 1-click payment option at Amazon, you can easily purchase books, magazines, and newspapers from Amazon, and automatically download your purchases to your Fire. Use these steps to purchase content:

1. At the top of the screen, tap the **Home** icon,

2. In the Navigation bar tap **Shop** to display the Amazon Kindle Store.

3. Browse among the various categories or search for items using the Search box at the upper right.

4. When the desired item appears, tap **Buy** to download the book or periodical, or tap **Try a Sample** to download the start of the book for free.

Once you purchase an item, it is stored in your own library in the Amazon Cloud, and you can download it to your Fire as well as any other Kindles that you may own. You can also read your purchases using any of the free Kindle Reader Apps available for most personal computers and smartphones.

Buying or renting movies or TV shows

The hassle-free way to purchase or rent movies or TV shows and watch them on your Fire is to do so using Amazon's Video store, since it is so tightly integrated with the device. You can rent videos, in which case you get to watch the video for a specified time period. (The clock doesn't begin ticking until you first begin watching the video.) Alternately, you can purchase a video, in which case you can watch it whenever you like. There are just three simple steps involved in choosing and watching a video from Amazon's Video Store on your Fire:

1. At the Home screen, swipe the main menu left or right as needed and tap **Video**.

2. If the video exists in your library, tap Library at the upper right, and locate and tap your video to begin playback.

3. If the video is not in your library, in the Search box, enter your video's title, **OR** swipe out from the screen's left edge to browse the Video store.

3. When you find the video you want, tap **Rent** or **Buy**.

For most movies and TV shows, you will see an option to purchase either standard definition or high definition. The cost of the rental or purchase gets charged to your 1-click billing account at Amazon.

NOTE: **Your video experience will be unacceptable without a high-speed internet connection.** Viewing movies or TV shows on your Fire (or on any tablet computer) requires the availability of a high-speed internet connection. If your internet speed is slow, you will see noticeable lags in your

46

video playback. Your home network should be providing at least 2 MB of download speed for standard definition, and 4 MB of download speed for high-definition video. If you are sufficiently fortunate to own one of the newer ultra-high definition TV sets, you are looking at a minimum of 15 MB of continuous download speed for streaming. (You can test your network's speed by going to a free speed testing site, such as www.speedtest.net.) Also, be aware that *each device* on a home network adds to the streaming workload. You may think that your ten-megabit high-speed connection from your local cable company should suffice. However, if two parents have an iPad and a Fire HDX, four kids have their own Fire H6 tablets, two of the neighbors' kids who are visiting have their own tablets and all eight devices are streaming from the same network at the same time, the network is badly overloaded.

TIP **Serious videophile? Consider Amazon Prime and / or Netflix.** If you are a major fan of watching movies and television shows, the author has two recommendations for you. The first is that you seriously consider becoming a member of Amazon Prime. For an annual fee of under $100 (at the time of this writing), in addition to the free two day shipping on a variety of items, you will also get to watch thousands of movies and shows from the Amazon Prime video library at no cost. Prime members can also stream movies and TV shows. The second recommendation is that you seriously consider a subscription to Netflix. You can then download the Netflix app at no cost from the Amazon AppStore, log into your Netflix account, and enjoy any one of the thousands of movies and shows available on Netflix.

Buying and downloading music from Amazon's Music Store

You can browse, shop for, and purchase your favorite music hits and download music from Amazon's Music Store using your Fire; the following three steps are all that's necessary. (If you're outside the United States, see the note at the end of this section.)

---

1. At the Home screen, tap **Music**, and then tap **Store**.

2. .If the song or album exists in your library, tap Library at the upper right, and locate and tap the desired song or album to begin playback.

3. If the song or album is not in your library, in the Search box, enter the title of the song or album, **OR** swipe out from the screen's left edge to browse the Music store, tap the button that displays the price, and confirm your purchase by tapping the Buy button. (In some cases, the songs are free, and if that is the case you will see a Get button. You can tap this button to get the song.)

TIP **Narrow your search to quickly find what you are looking for.** You can narrow your search by swiping out from the left side of the screen and then tapping Bestsellers, New Releases, or Browse Genres.

TIP **Try before you buy.** If you want to listen to a sample of a song before purchasing the song, tap the 'Play' link (a triangle within a circle) beside the song's title. You'll hear a 30 second sample of the song.

Once you purchase a song or music album, it is in your account in the Amazon Cloud. You can download a song to your Fire at any time, by going to your Home page, tapping Music, tapping Cloud, and locating the desired song or album. Do a long-press (press and hold) on the song title or album cover until a popup menu appears, then choose 'Download' from the popup menu to download the song to your device.

NOTE: Copyright laws regarding music very from nation to nation. In order to buy music from Amazon's US-based Music store, you must have an Amazon account, a United States billing address, and a 1-click payment method that's been issued by a U.S. bank. And if you're using an Amazon gift card to make purchases, you must be physically located in the United States to use the Amazon Music Store. Amazon customers located within the United Kingdom can access the UK based Music store by going to www.amazon.co.uk and clicking the Music link.

Removing content from your device

If you are done with a particular book, magazine, or video, you can remove the item from your Fire. Use these steps to remove an item from your Fire:

1. Press **Home**.
2. At the Home screen, perform a 'long press' on the icon for the item.
3. At the popup menu that appears, choose **'Remove from Device.'**

The item remains in your personal space within the Amazon cloud, so you can always download the same item at a later time if you would like to again view the content.

Getting Kindle Books from your local library (without setting foot in your library)

Borrow Kindle content for free from your public library. Many Kindle owners are oblivious to the fact that most public libraries now loan books, movies, music, and other digital content for the Amazon Kindle line of e-readers (as well as for other digital products like smartphones, Apple iPads, and other tablet computers.) In the United States alone, at the time of this writing, nearly 20,000 public libraries are members of a system called OverDrive Media. OverDrive Media provides an app for your Fire that lets you borrow content electronically from your public library. All you'll need is the app (a free download from the Amazon store) and your library card number. Check with your local library to see if they are a member of the OverDrive program. You should be able to check without getting out of your easy chair; do a Google search for your town's public library web site, and once you find it, look for a link that says "download e-books" or something similar. If your city does not have a membership in such a program, there are libraries that allow nonresidents to obtain a library card for an annual fee. Two, at the time of this writing, are those of Fairfax County, Virginia (www.fairfaxcounty.gov/library for more information) and the City of Philadelphia (www.freelibrary.org for more information).

Once you've found that your library is a member of the OverDrive Media service, go to the Amazon App store, search on the term 'overdrive', and download the app to your Fire. Launch the app, and you'll be asked for a ZIP code; enter your zip code, and you'll see your local library's name in a list. Select your library by name, and you'll be taken to a page for your local library, where you can borrow books, movies, and other digital content. Browse among what your library has available for lending, click on a title, and you'll be taken to an Amazon page with the book, but in place of the "Buy with one click" button, you'll see a "Borrow from library" button. Click that button, and the book will be downloaded to your Fire.

Different libraries have different lending policies, so you'll want to check with your local library to determine the exact length of your loan. In my resident town of Charlotte, North Carolina, books have a two-week loan with one possible renewal, and movies are good for ten days. Many libraries now offer regularly scheduled classes or workshops that teach library patrons how to download digital content, so you may want to visit your local library and sign up for such a class in your home town.

Using the Kindle Owner's Lending Library ("KOLL") to your advantage

The second great free source of books is Amazon's own Kindle Owners Lending Library. If you are a member of Amazon Prime, you owe it to yourself to check out the Kindle Owners' Lending Library. The Kindle Owners Lending Library allows Amazon Prime members to borrow one book at a time each month, at no cost. There are thousands of books available through the service, and you can find free books to borrow through the Kindle Owners Lending Library using these steps:

1. At the Fire store, click "See all categories." When the list of various categories (Books, Kindle Singles, Kindle Newsstand, New & Noteworthy, etc.) appears, click the Kindle Owners' Lending Library option.

2. After picking the Kindle Owners' Lending Library, you can browse a list of books to borrow. You will know that a book is eligible for borrowing because it will have a "Prime" badge attached.

3. Click the 'Borrow' tab. Next, you'll see a "Buy for $xx.xx" tab and a "Borrow for Free" tab. Click the "Borrow for Free" tab, and your borrowed book will be downloaded to your Fire.

Easily Search the Kindle Store for Free Books

A third great way to find free books is to search for... free books! As part of regular ongoing promotions, many authors will place their books on sale at no cost during certain days of a 90-day period, as part of an authors' program called Amazon KDP Select. You can take advantage of this fact by simply searching among any desired genre of Kindle books, and entering "0.00" as your search criteria in the Search box. What appears will be every Kindle book that has a price of zero dollars, zero cents on that particular day. (And before you think that checking this list would result in a limited selection, you should know that on any given day there are hundreds of free books offered through Amazon's promotional program.) This list of books will change wildly on a daily basis, so if you're an avid reader, you may find it worth your while to perform this sort of a search on a regular basis.

+ip! **Download free books from the Internet, and transfer these to your Fire using your USB cable.** The final source of free books that this chapter will detail is that of the Internet itself. You can find countless sources of free e-books on the Internet. These come in a variety of file formats; besides its own native file format of Kindle (.azw) files, your Fire will also read books in Adobe Acrobat (.PDF) format, in MobiPocket (.MOBI) format, or in plain text (.TXT) format. Unfortunately, your Fire will NOT read files in the popular E-PUB format used by the Sony e-reader, the Barnes and Noble NOOK, and many other e-readers. The solution for this is not overwhelmingly complex; you can download free e-book converter programs that will convert e-books from most other formats into Amazon's Kindle (.KZW) format. An excellent program is called Calibre (go to www.calibre-ebook.com for details). Calibre can convert files from many formats, including the E-PUB format, into the Amazon Kindle file format. Once you convert the file, use the file transfer techniques described in Chapter 5 of this book, to transfer the e-books that you've converted to your Fire.

As for sources, performing a Google search for "free e-books" will return an avalanche of sites. Here is a small list to get you started:

Project Gutenberg- www.gutenberg.org

ManyBooks.net- http://manybooks.net

Google Books- http://books.google.com/

MobiPocket Free Books-
www.mobipocket.com/freebooks/

An exhaustive source of free computer-based books can be found at http://freecomputerbooks.com. Finally, you'll find a surprisingly comprehensive list of textbooks that can be legally shared, at http://textbookrevolution.org. These are in .PDF format.

Chapter 4: Silk browser tips, tricks, and traps

The Amazon Silk web browser for the Fire is unique among web browsers, engineered from the ground up especially for the Fire. Since Android-based tablets will certainly run established browsers such as Google Chrome and Mozilla Firefox, many have wondered why Amazon chose to design a new browser from scratch. The answer is, Amazon wanted to offer a fast browsing experience, so the browser design splits tasks between the browser software that is running locally on the Fire, and Amazon's Cloud Servers. As a result of this unique design, a number of features are familiar to you because you've seen them in other browsers, but there are a few that are unique to the Silk browser.

Check out the Amazon Help Video.

Amazon has taken the time to provide a short help video about the Silk browser. At the Amazon web site, tap or click 'Help' (just below the Search box), and at the next page, under 'Browse Help Topics' select 'Amazon devices' and at the right, choose 'Fire HD8' or 'Fire HD10' as is appropriate. Under 'Fire tablet apps,' tap or click 'Silk browser.'

Surfing the Web with the Silk Browser

To launch the Silk browser, at the Home screen, swipe up from the bottom of the screen to display your apps, and tap the Silk browser icon (shown here).

Silk browser

The following illustration shows the parts of the Silk browser.

Menu (recently viewed, book-marks, browser settings)

URL / search string

Refresh

Back

Bookmarks

Add tab

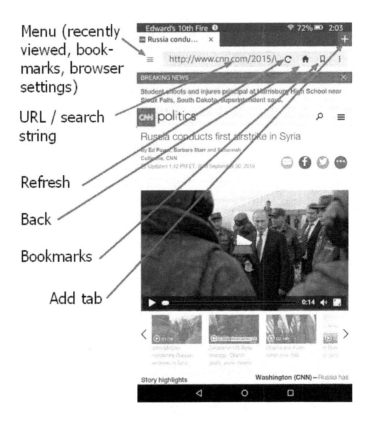

The Silk browser is a tabbed browser, like Google's Chrome, Mozilla Firefox, and Microsoft Edge. To open a new tab, just tap the plus sign in the top right corner. You can then tap in the Search field and enter the desired web address.

If you are viewing a page and there is a link embedded in the page and you would like to go to that link in a separate tab, give the link a long press rather than a tap. A menu of options will appear, and you can choose 'Open in new tab' from the menu.

Share web pages with your friends.
When a page is displayed in the Silk browser, the Quick menu button at the right of the URL/search box will include a Share Page symbol. Tap this option, and you can send a link to the page either via email, or through Facebook or Twitter.

The "thumb and finger spread" or "thumb and finger pinch" works in the Silk browser. You will often encounter web pages with text that is too small to read on the Fire screen. Place your thumb and finger on the screen and spread them to magnify, or pinch them together to reduce the magnification.

Let the browser complete your entry. As you begin typing characters into the search / address field, a list of suggestions appears below the field. Type more characters, and suggestions increase in accuracy. When you see a suggestion that matches the URL you intended to type, tap that suggestion.

Using Bookmarks

Bookmark commonly visited pages so you can return to them quickly at a later time. As with all modern web browsers, the Silk browser provides the ability to bookmark sites so that you can easily return to the same site. To add a bookmark, tap the Quick Menu icon at the right of the URL/search box and in the menu that opens, tap Add Bookmark to reveal the Add Bookmarks dialog box. Change the name of the entry to something friendlier if you desire, and tap OK, to add the page to your bookmarked pages.

Quickly get to your bookmarked pages. There are different ways to go to a bookmarked page, but this method seems to involve the least amount of steps. Tap the Menu icon at the top left and drag the Silk sidebar out. Tap Bookmarks, locate the desired bookmark, and tap the bookmark to open that webpage.

Delete any bookmark page that's no longer needed. From the Bookmarks page (get there by tapping the Menu icon at the top left, dragging the Silk sidebar out, and tapping Bookmarks), perform a long-press on the unwanted bookmark, and choose "Delete Bookmark" from the menu that appears.

Changing Silk Settings for Best Operation

Choose your preferred search engine. The default search engine for the Silk browser is Google, but if you prefer to use Microsoft Bing or Yahoo as your default search engine, you can change the Silk browser to either of these options. With a browser page open, swipe out from the left edge and tap Settings, tap Search Engine, and make your desired choice.

Keep Silk performance up through regular housecleaning. Just as browsers on your PC can be slowed over time from too many cookies or from a clogged cache, so can the Silk browser. You can perform a bit of browser housecleaning on occasion. With a browser page open, swipe out from the left edge, tap Settings and under 'Advanced Settings,' tap Privacy. At the next screen that appears, tap Clear Browsing Data and confirm the option when asked.

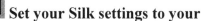 **Set your Silk settings to your preferences**. The Silk browser has a number of settings that you can use to change the operation of the browser. With a browser window open, swipe out from the left edge, OR tap the Menu icon at the upper left (it's the set of three horizontal bars just to the left of the URL/Search box. In the panel that opens, tap Settings. You will see the settings that apply to the browser, as shown in the following illustration.

(Silk browser settings, Fire tablet)

These settings affect the way the Silk Browser behaves in various ways. In addition to selecting your desired choice of search engine, you can also choose whether or not you want to display the most recent page visited within the carousel, and whether you want to clear the history, the cache, and accept cookies or clear cookie data from the browser. You also have options to remember passwords used when visiting sites, to clear all passwords from the browser memory, and whether or not to remember form data or to clear form data. You can enable location tracking or clear location access, and under Advanced Settings, you can choose whether images are normally loaded, whether JavaScript is enabled, and whether security warnings are enabled.

Chapter 5: File Management Tips, Tricks and Traps

In press reviews, Amazon's Fire tablet product line has taken a fair share of criticism for being a relatively "closed ecosystem," according to its critics. Many reviewers have claimed that Fire owners are dependent on purchasing virtually all content from Amazon. In the opinion of this author, that reputation is somewhat undeserved. Certainly, it is in Amazon's interest to get you to buy your content from Amazon. But the 'closed ecosystem' claim made by many members of the press implies that you must purchase all your content from Amazon, and that is simply not the case. In addition to purchasing content from the Amazon store, you can find millions (literally!) of books from other sources, and these can be copied to your Fire from your computer using the USB cable that is a part of your charging assembly. The Fire uses the .mobi file format for its e-books, and e-books in the .mobi format can be found in thousands of places all over the internet, some paid, and others free. There are also millions of books in the popular E-PUB format used by Sony and by Google, and there are free converters readily available from hundreds of sources on the web that will convert files from the E-PUB format into the .mobi format used by all Amazon Kindles.

You can use the same USB cable techniques to copy MP3, AAC, or WAV files that you obtain from your own sources, and these become a part of the music library on your Fire. There are apps like Crackle that let you stream any one of thousands of free movies or TV shows to your Fire. If you are already a Netflix subscriber, you can download the Netflix app from the Amazon app store (the app is free) and watch any content that you would normally obtain from Netflix on your Fire. And short length, personal movies compatible with the Fire (in 3gp or mp4 format) can also be copied to the device, although the 8 gigabyte memory size is by nature going to limit the length of movies that can be stored locally on the device. (By comparison, an average Blu-ray DVD occupies 25 gigabytes of disk space.)

You can also email documents directly to your Fire, using Amazon's free Send to Kindle service. Every registered Kindle has its own assigned email address, and you can send certain types of files- Microsoft Word documents, rich text (RTF) or text (TXT) files, .JPG or .PNG graphics files, Adobe PDF files, and others- to your Fire's assigned email address. (See the following heading if you do not know your Fire's assigned e-mail address.) Within roughly 5 minutes of the time that you send a file as an attachment, it will show up on your Fire, in the Documents folder. You can then tap the document to open it and read it in the native Kindle Viewer, and there are apps available that will let you edit Microsoft Word documents on your Kindle.

To take full advantage of all of these features of the Fire, you'll need to know how to use the file management features of the Fire. You'll find the various tips, tricks, and traps that pertain to these topics covered throughout this chapter.

Sending Files to your Fire via E-mail

Know your Fire's email address. If you purchased your Fire directly from Amazon, it was registered for you when it arrived. If you purchased it from a retailer such as Best Buy, you may have gone through the setup steps on your own. In either case, your Fire has been assigned a Send to Kindle email address. This address is something similar to *username@kindle.com*. To see your email address, swipe down from the top of the screen, tap Setting, and under Settings, tap My Account. You will see a message that reads something like-

Edward's second Kindle is registered to Edward
Jones

edjones45@kindle.com

This is the email address that you can use to send files
as attachments to your Fire.

**Before you can send any documents
to your Fire, you must add the sending email address to an
"Approved personal document email list" under your
Amazon account settings**. To prevent Kindle owners from
receiving unwanted spam, Amazon blocks any email sent to a
Kindle address at Kindle.com that hasn't been added to the
approved personal document email list. Log into your Amazon
account in a computer's web browser, and under the 'Your
Account' link, click 'Manage Your Kindle.' At the next screen
that appears, you'll see all your Kindle devices (assuming you
own more than one). If you own just one Fire, you will see
just that device. Scroll down and locate the desired Kindle in
your list of devices, click the Edit link to the right of the
device name, and you will be able to change the e-mail
address registered to that Kindle. You can also add authorized
e-mail addresses that will be permitted to send e-mail to your
Kindle. By default, Amazon adds the e-mail address that is
associated with your Amazon account. To add authorized
addresses, under 'Your Kindle Account' at the left, click
Personal Document Settings, and then look for the Approved
Personal Document E-mail List near the bottom of the screen.
You can click the 'Add a new Approved E-mail Address' link
in this area to add another email address.

Once you've added your email address to the approved personal document email list, you can attach files to an email message and send it to your send to kindle address. Documents can be in the form of .DOC, .DOCX, .RTF, .TXT, .HTM or .HTML, ZIP, .MOBI' and .AZW file formats. Images can be sent in the .JPG, .PNG, .GIF, or .BMP file formats. The conversion process assumes an active Wi-Fi connection, since Amazon's Send to Kindle service converts your file into Amazon's own .AZW file format, then downloads it to your Fire using Amazon's Whispernet.

Attachments cannot be larger than 50 megabytes per attachment, and each email must not have more than 25 attachments. If any of your files are larger than 50 megabytes, the Send to Kindle process will fail for that file, and that file will not appear in your Documents folder.

Use the Send to Kindle service to convert PDF files to Amazon readable documents. In addition to the file types listed in the previous tip, you can also send PDF files to your Kindle, and Amazon uses a conversion service to convert the PDF file into Amazon's own .AZW file format. Simply add the word "convert" to the subject line of your email, then attach the PDF file and send the email to your Send to Kindle email address.

Transferring Files to your Fire with its Charging Cable

You can also transfer files from a laptop or desktop computer to your Fire, using a USB to micro-USB cable. This is the same type of cable that is supplied as a charging cable for your Fire; one end contains the micro USB connector that plugs into the base of your Fire, and the other end contains a standard USB connector. Use the cable to connect your Fire to your computer, and the Fire will appear as a USB flash drive under your computer's operating system.

Users of Windows XP may have to install additional software before using a USB cable to access the Fire, and the users of the Apple Mac will have to install additional software. Go to the following link for additional details:

http://www.kindle.com/support/downloads

Once the Fire appears as a USB drive under your computer's operating system, you can simply drag and drop or copy and paste the desired files into the appropriate folders of the Fire.

When connected to your computer, a Fire tablet resembles a flash drive.

Note the DOCUMENTS, PICTURES, and MUSIC folders. You'll probably copy content into these folders most often.

You can use a USB cable to transfer files in the form of .DOC, .DOCX, .XLS, .PPT, .RTF, .TXT, .HTM or .HTML, ZIP, .MOBI' and .AZW file formats. Images can be in the .JPG, .PNG, .GIF, or .BMP file formats, and audio files can be in the .AAC, .MP3, .MIDI, .OGG, or .WAV file formats.

Transferring Files Wirelessly with the Wi-Fi File Explorer App

You can transfer files to your Fire wirelessly ('look ma, no cables!') Assuming you have a home network with PCs attached to it, you don't necessarily have to resort to the annoyance of a cable connected between your Fire and your computer every time you want to move a file between the two. Wi-Fi File Explorer is a neat little app that lets you transfer files wirelessly. Download and install this free app on your Fire, and when you run the app, once you identify the Wi-Fi network used by the Fire, you'll see a display giving you a web address that you can point a browser on any computer that's also on your network. The address will include a port number, similar to the following:

http://192.168.1.15:8000

Point your computer's web browser to the address you're given (yours will likely differ from this example) and you'll see a display like the following:

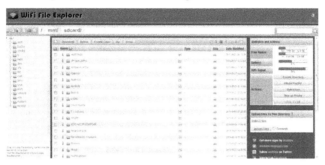

Wi-Fi File Explorer gives you a file explorer view of all the folders on your Fire. You can drill down into any folder, and use the Download button at the top of the Wi-Fi File Explorer window to move files from your laptop to your Fire, without the hassle of wires.

Adding file storage space with a Micro SD Ram Card

You can greatly increase the available storage space for personal files by adding an optional micro SD RAM card to your Fire. The addition of a micro SD RAM card will provide plenty of room for space-consuming items like personal videos or thousands of .mp3 music files. The Fire supports the use of micro SDHC cards of up to 128GB in size. You can add a micro SD ram card using the following steps:

1. Completely power down your Fire by pressing and holding the power button for 10 seconds. When the turn off power prompt appears on the screen, tap power off.

2. Place your Fire face down on a cushioned surface, and determine where the micro SD Ram slot is located on your model of Fire. When viewed from the rear, the micro SD Ram slot is located at the upper left edge, just below the rear-facing camera.

3. Locate the small protective cover over the micro SD card slot. Using your finger tip, gently pull the cover open, turning it to one side to reveal the slot, as shown in the previous illustration.

4. Hold the memory card gently between your thumb and forefinger, with the logo facing the front (screen side) of the tablet. Gently guide the card into the slot.

5. Push gently against the card, guiding it into the slot until it clicks into place.

6. Close the protective cover and snap it into place.

7. Turn on your Fire tablet.

When you add an SD Ram card and turn on your Fire tablet, you'll see the following message informing you that videos, photos, and apps will now be stored to the SD Ram card. As the message states, any content stored on the SD Ram card will only be available when the SD Ram card is present in the Fire tablet.

Expanded Storage

Videos, photos, and apps will now be stored to your SD Card. To make changes, go to Settings. Note that content saved or downloaded to the SD Card is only accessible if the SD Card is inserted.

SETTINGS   OK

When an SD Ram card is present in a Fire tablet, additional options appear under the Device menu of Settings. Swipe down from the top of the screen, tap Settings, and at the Next screen, tap Device and then tap Storage. You will see the following options that are not present unless an SD Ram card has been inserted.

If you add an SD Ram card to increase the storage capacity of your Fire, you may find it helpful to add a third-party file management app to your apps collection. The Fire (and other Android-based tablets) automatically scan and display media content in the photos, videos, and music apps you use, but if you want to access the files and folders directly, you must work with a file management app. There are a number of file management apps available for your Fire, and many of these apps provide more flexibility and added capabilities. This author likes ES File Explorer due to its flexibility and its clear, consistent user interface. If you're interested, search the Amazon AppStore under 'Apps' for the search term "ES File Explorer."

Chapter 6: Email Tips, Tricks, and Traps

One of the many capabilities of the Fire centers on the email client that is built into the device. All of the basic features that you would expect to find in an email client are here; you can open and read mail, reply to and compose mail, download attachments, and send email with attached files. The latest models of the Fire add significant improvements to the built-in e-mail client. Clearly Amazon engineering has been paying attention to user feedback, because the e-mail client that was mediocre at best in the first generation Fires has improved to a level of capable, in this author's opinion. The e-mail app now supports labeling, threaded conversations, and archiving of emails for offline reading. Integrated calendar support of both Google's Gmail and Microsoft Exchange are additional welcome features.

Check out the Amazon Help Video.

Amazon has taken the time to provide a short help video on the subject of e-mail. At the Amazon web site, tap or click 'Help' (just below the Search box), and at the next page, under 'Browse Help Topics' select 'Amazon devices' and at the right, choose 'Fire HD8' or 'Fire HD10' as is appropriate. Under 'Fire tablet apps,' tap or click the 'Email' link.

Setting up your Fire E-mail

You can set up most email accounts quickly with Auto-configuration. If you're like many individuals, you probably have a number of e-mail accounts. With your Fire, you can stay on top of your e-mail from anywhere. Later sections of this chapter will delve into using e-mail on the Fire in greater detail, but for now, you may find the great auto-configuration feature is all you need to get your multiple e-mail accounts up and running. The feature works with e-mail accounts provided by Google (Gmail), Yahoo Mail, AOL Mail, Microsoft Live Mail (formerly known as Hotmail), Microsoft's Outlook.com, Apple's iCloud Mail, and BT Internet (United Kingdom). Use the following steps to set up your e-mail account on your Fire:

1. From the Home ⌂ screen, tap Apps in the Menu bar.

2. Swipe upwards from the bottom of the screen to see the apps on your device,

3. Tap the Email app icon (shown here).

Assuming you've never setup an email account on your Fire, the Add Account screen will appear, as shown in the following illustration. (If an e-mail account has been set up on your device and you want to add another, drag down from the top of the screen, and tap Settings > Applications >Email, Contacts, Calendar > Add Account.)

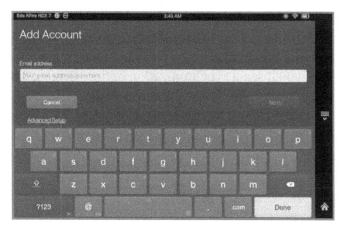

(Tap any image to enlarge the image.)

Enter your e-mail address and then tap Next. You may now see a sign-in screen for Google, Yahoo, AOL, Microsoft Live or Outlook Mail, or iCloud, depending on your choice of e-mail providers, or you may see a screen asking for your password. (An example of the sign-in screen presented to users of Google's Gmail is shown in the following illustration.)

Enter any requested information, and your Fire will attempt to connect the new email account settings with the servers of your email account provider. Once it successfully does so, you'll see a synchronization options screen, similar to the one shown in the following illustration:

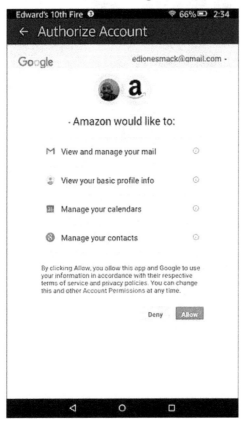

This screen asks for permission to synchronize your contacts and calendar on your Fire with that of your e-mail provider. Tap Accept, and in a moment, you should see a screen indicating a successful setup of your e-mail account.

Fire receives incoming emails, but is unable to send outgoing emails. After setup of an email account, some users report that they are able to receive emails, but can't send mail. The problem is usually that when you fill in the setup screen, the Fire assumes that your username is also your outgoing SMTP address setting. And this is true with most providers, but not with all providers. As an example, if your email provider is Comcast cable, and your full email address is *johndoe@comcast.net*, when going through the setup screen, you probably entered *johndoe* when prompted for a user name. As a result, the Fire's email client is trying to send out email with an SMTP address setting of *johndoe*, when the setting should be *johndoe@comcast.net*. To solve the problem, go back into the email settings you have on your Fire, and enter the entire outgoing email address manually. (For details on how to do this, see the following topic.)

Setting up E-mail manually

The automated e-mail setup on the Fire does a great job when it works, but it does not always work, and when it fails to work, you'll need to set up your e-mail manually. Before starting a manual e-mail account setup process, there is some information that you will want to make sure that you have from your e-mail service provider. Of course, you will need to know your e-mail address and the password for the account. In addition, you will need to know the server settings of your mail server. You will need the SMTP settings, as well as either the POP or the IMAP settings. (The SMTP setting is used for sending mail, and POP and IMAP are both used for receiving mail. IMAP is a newer standard for receiving mail, so if your mail server supports both POP and IMAP, use the IMAP settings.) Finally, you will need to know the security type used by the servers, and the default incoming and outgoing ports. (You should be able to obtain all of this information from your e-mail provider.) Once you've obtained the information, perform the following steps to manually set up an e-mail account on the Fire:

1. If no e-mail accounts currently exist on your device, tap Apps, then tap the E-mail icon.

2. At the next screen, tap Create E-mail account. If one or more e-mail accounts already exist on your device, drag down the Navigation bar and tap Settings, and then tap Applications > Email, Contacts, Calendar.

3. At the next screen that appears, tap Add Account.

4. Enter your e-mail address and password where prompted, and then tap Next. You will see an Add Account screen asking you to choose the type of account, as shown in the following illustration.

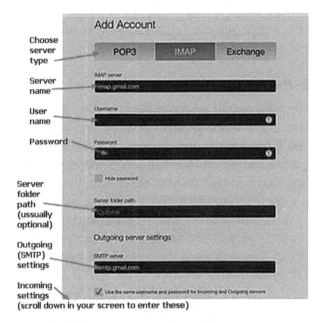

5. Select the type of email account you are creating. (Your available choices are a POP3 account, an IMAP account, or a Microsoft Exchange Account. The remainder of this topic will help you with the common POP3 and IMAP types; if you are setting up a Microsoft Exchange-hosted account, see the following topic for details.

6. Next, you will be asked to provide your incoming server settings. These will include your user name, password, POP3 or IMAP server address, security type, port number, and

the desired 'delete email from server' setting. Enter this information, then tap Done at the bottom of the screen.

Your Fire will attempt to connect to the Incoming server with the settings you supplied. If the connection is successful, the Outgoing server settings screen will appear.

7. Enter your outgoing server settings. These will include your user name, password, SMTP server address, security type (if any), port number, and whether the server will require a sign-in. After entering this information, tap Next.

8. The first time you connect, you will be asked to give this mail account a unique on-screen name, and you will need to supply your name. (The e-mail app uses the unique account name to differentiate the account from all other email accounts on your Fire.) Touch Done, and your manually created e-mail account is ready for use.

NOTE: Manual setups of e-mail accounts can be tricky, to say the least. You are required to enter a number of values, and if any single value is incorrect, your e-mail works partially, or does not work at all. If you are unsuccessful in setting up your e-mail account, try changing the entry in the 'username' field to your full e-mail address. Some systems expect to see your full e-mail address (such as 'johndoe@carolinarr.timewarnercable.com'), and other systems only want to see the username ('such as 'johndoe'). If you've tried both formats with no success, it's probably time to get as many details about the settings as possible from your e-mail provider, and then punch that 'Help' button on your Fire, and find the current phone number for Amazon technical support.

Reading your E-Mail

The e-mail client that is provided with your Fire does all that you would expect of a solid e-mail client. You can read, compose, and send emails, and you can add attachments to those emails. You can also read e-mails that contain attachments of many file types, including pictures, video attachments, Adobe .PDF attachments, and Microsoft office document attachments. The e-mail client also integrates with the Contacts app that is built into the Fire, so you can send e-mails to contacts that you enter in your contacts directory.

You perform most common mail-related tasks from your Inbox. To get to your Inbox, tap Apps, then locate and tap the Email icon, shown here.

Your Inbox opens, displaying your mail in a fashion similar to that shown here, assuming that you are in landscape view. (If you are in portrait view, you will only see either the message list or the contents of the message at one time, so you may want to switch to landscape view for best reading by rotating the Fire.)

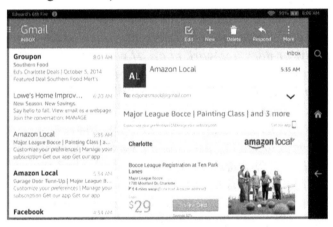

(Tap any image to enlarge the image.)

To read an e-mail, just open the Inbox, and tap the desired mail item in the list at the left to open the mail. When you do so, its content will appear in the active portion of the screen, at the right.

78

Switching between multiple mail accounts

If you've set up more than one e-mail account, you can switch by tapping the Menu icon (at the top left corner of the E-mail screen). An e-mail sidebar will open, and you can tap the inbox name for the account you want to check.

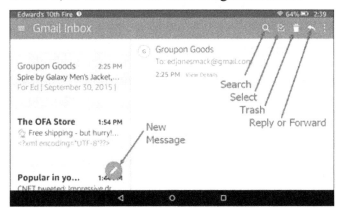 The Fire e-mail app has a nice feature called the **combined inbox**, which displays mail from multiple accounts simultaneously (assuming that you have set up more than one e-mail account on your device). Tap the Menu icon (at the top left corner of the E-mail screen), and choose Combined Inbox from the sidebar that opens. Once you do this, you will see all messages from all established accounts within a single list.

Composing and Sending Mail

Writing email is also a straightforward process. Use these steps to compose a new e-mail:

At the Home screen tap Apps, then tap the E-Mail icon to get into the e-mail app. When your Inbox opens, note the toolbar that appears at the upper right as well as the New Message icon that appears within the lower left area of the window, as shown in the following illustration.

(Tap any image to enlarge the image.)

Using the toolbar buttons and the New Message icon, you can compose a new e-mail, reply to an e-mail, or delete an e-mail from your Inbox.

Once in the e-mail app, tap the New Message icon to display a New Message screen (shown here).

To, Cc, and Subject fields

Message text here

Enter the recipient's e-mail address in the To box. (Alternately, you can tap the Contacts icon and choose an address that's in your Contacts list.) When entering multiple names, separate any additional names with commas. (You can also use the Cc: and Bcc: fields to add copied recipients and blind copied recipients, respectively.)

In the Subject area, enter a subject for the message, and then enter the desired message text in the Message area. You can add attachments (such as photos stored on your Fire) by tapping the More menu (the three vertical dots) at the right side of the message. When you tap this icon, the menu shown here opens, and you can choose Attach a Photo, Attach File, or Capture a Photo from the menu. (If you choose Attach a Photo, you can select an image stored in the \Pictures folder of your Fire, while choosing Attach File lets you select a file that is stored in your \Documents folder of your Fire. Choose Capture a Photo to take a photo using one of the built-in cameras of the Fire, and immediately send that photo as an attachment.

When done composing your message and adding any necessary attachments, tap the Send icon in the upper-right portion of the toolbar to send your message.

Customize your E-mail operation with various settings

Speed up your email performance by hiding images. If you receive a large amount of email that contains embedded images, display of your messages can be slowed by the presence of the images. You can turn off the display of embedded images by default. Pull down the Navigation bar, tap Settings, tap Device, and under Apps and Games, within the 'Amazon Applications' subcategory, tap 'Email, Contacts, Calendar. At the next screen that appears, tap Email Settings. You will a screen similar to the following:

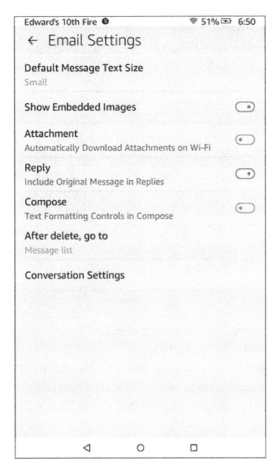

← Email Settings

Default Message Text Size
Small

Show Embedded Images

Attachment
Automatically Download Attachments on Wi-Fi

Reply
Include Original Message in Replies

Compose
Text Formatting Controls in Compose

After delete, go to
Message list

Conversation Settings

Show embedded images is normally on by default at this screen. Set this option to Off to speed up your mail performance.

Add a custom signature to save typing time. You can add a default signature line to the bottom of your outgoing messages, to save yourself the time involved in having to sign every letter that you compose. To do this, drag down the Navigation bar and tap Settings, then at the Settings screen, tap Applications, then tap Email/Contacts/Calendar, and then tap Email Settings. At the next screen that appears select the desired email account by name, scroll down within the dialog box, tap Signature, and enter the desired personal signature.

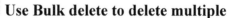 **Use Bulk delete to delete multiple messages.** There is no need to delete messages one at a time if you want to delete a group of messages. Just turn on the checkboxes at the left of all of the unwanted messages, and tap the Delete icon (it appears in the shape of a trash can) at the top of the screen to delete the selected messages as a group.

Using your synchronized calendars and contacts

Once you've set up your e-mail accounts, assuming that you allow synchronization of calendars and contacts with your e-mail accounts, you will also be able to use the Calendar and Contacts apps built into your Fire. At the Home screen, tap Apps, then tap Calendar. A view of a synchronized calendar from your Google, Microsoft, iCloud, or Yahoo account will appear (the illustration that follows shows an example of a synchronized calendar based on a Google account).

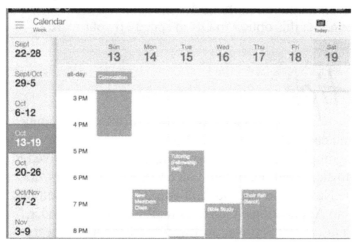

You can make changes or additions to your calendar by tapping within any date and time field, and then tapping the Plus (+) symbol that appears. A New Event screen will appear as shown in the following illustration, and you can enter the details about your calendar event.

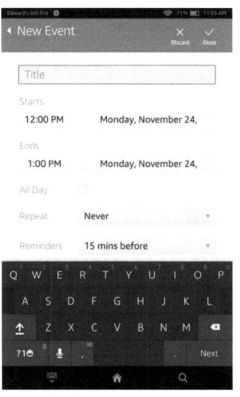

To see your synchronized contacts list, get to the Home screen, tap Apps, and locate and tap the Contacts icon. A synchronized contacts list will appear; the following illustration shows an example of a Contacts list based on a Google account. (And yes, the author does have a fondness for dead presidents, particularly the ones depicted on greenbacks, but that is another story.)

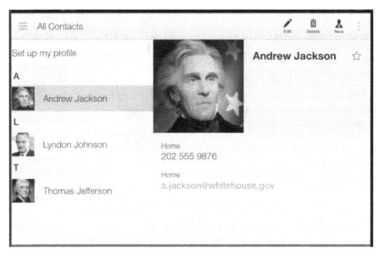

Set up my profile

A

Andrew Jackson

L

Lyndon Johnson

T

Thomas Jefferson

Andrew Jackson ☆

Home
202 555 9876

Home
a.jackson@whitehouse.gov

When viewing any contact, you can use the toolbar buttons that appear at the upper-right to edit an existing contact in your list, to delete a contact, or to add a new contact. As with the calendar, since the accounts are synchronized with those of your e-mail provider, any changes that you make using your Fire will be entered in the cloud-based contacts list provided by your e-mail provider.

Consider using an optional app as your Email client. While the Email client that is built into the Fire does an acceptable job, you should be aware that this is not your only option for managing email. There are apps available from the Amazon AppStore, some of them free that serve as perfectly acceptable alternatives to the Fire's built-in e-mail app. One that this author particularly likes is SkitM@il, by SkitApps.

SkitM@il is a full-featured e-mail client that supports multiple mailboxes on the Fire. If you are like many wired individuals, you probably have multiple mailboxes from different providers. Perhaps you have one address with

Yahoo, another with Google's Gmail, the third for a domain associated with your job, and a fourth associated with a cell phone carrier. Chances are, all your accounts support universal Internet mail protocol standards such as POP or IMAP. If that's the case, you can consolidate all your messages from multiple accounts into one place, with SkitM@il.

SkitM@il has everything you'd expect in a full featured e-mail client; automatic e-mail push (meaning, incoming e-mail messages appear in SkitM@il as they are received), access to synchronized messages when you are offline, and multiple folders for synchronization. From the main screen, all your e-mail accounts appear under the names that you create for them. Once you've added a new e-mail account, all of the folders associated with that account-- all mail, drafts, sent mail, and trash-- become accessible. Besides all the usual features found in an e-mail client (compose new messages, reply, forward, and delete), you can also move messages into folders, and "star" the messages for later review when you are offline. SkitM@il also lets you sort your mail in a number of different ways. You can sort your mail by date, by subjects, by sender, or by attachment type.

SkitM@il's display is also highly customizable, which is a big plus over the default mail client that comes with the Fire. You can change the default font size and the styles used to suit your tastes. SkitM@il is simple to install, setup, and use; it supports POP, IMAP, and Microsoft Exchange (with WebDAV); and it stands a cut above the default e-mail that comes with the Fire just in terms of its flexibility.

Chapter 7: Multimedia Tips, Tricks, and Traps

One of the major strengths of the Fire centers on its impressive multimedia capabilities. Designed to provide you with a better multimedia experience, the Fire is small enough to hold in your hand, yet delivers a vibrant viewing experience with over 16 million colors on its high definition screen. The sharp, beautiful color display is backed by dual stereo speakers built into the device, along with support for Dolby sound. For the technically inclined, the Fire supports 3gp and mp4 video formats, H264 video encoding, with an 800 by 480 resolution and a 2500 kps bit rate. On the audio side, the Fire HP supports AAC, MP3, MIDI, OGG, and WAV formats, and uses AAC for audio encoding of movies' audio tracks.

Playing personal videos on your Fire

 **Play your personal videos on your Fire**. You can transfer video files or download video files and play them on your Fire. You cannot place them in the video library, but you can copy your personal videos into the /Pictures subfolder of your Fire (and no, "/Pictures" is not a misprint). Your videos will appear alongside your photos when you tap Photos on the Navigation bar. The only visual difference between your photos and your videos will be the presence of an arrow within a circle, like this:

which acts as a "Play" button for the video player. Tap the arrow, and your video will begin playing on your Fire's screen.

You can copy files that are stored in the 3GP or MP4 video format into the /Pictures folder that appears in the directory of folders shown on your computer when the Fire is connected by means of the USB cable. When you connect the Fire to the micro USB side of the charging cable and connect the standard USB side of the cable to your computers USB port, the Fire appears on your computer's File Explorer or file management system as a USB flash drive, similar to the example shown in the following illustration.

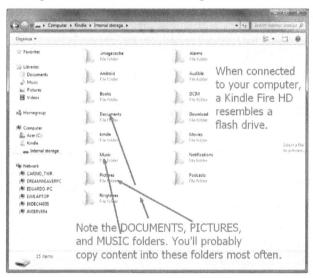

When connected to your computer, a Kindle Fire HD resembles a flash drive.

Note the DOCUMENTS, PICTURES, and MUSIC folders. You'll probably copy content into these folders most often.

You can then use standard cut / copy / paste or drag-and-drop procedures to copy the video file from the source folder that contains the video file on your hard drive to the destination folder that appears with all the other folders of your Kindle's internal storage under the device name 'Kindle.'

You can copy your photos, images, or personal video files into the /Pictures folder, and these will appear within a tiled directory style view when you tap Photos in the Navigation bar on your Home screen. In a similar fashion, you can copy .mp3 files into the /Music subfolder, and these will appear as songs when you tap Music in the Navigation bar. You can copy Microsoft Word documents, rich text format (.RTF) files, and text (.TXT) files into the /Documents folder, and these will appear when you tap Documents in the Navigation bar.

A file may exist in the acceptable file format of 3GP or MP4, yet may refuse to play on a Fire. Not only must the files be stored as a 3GP or MP4 format, the length by width (800 by 480) and video bitrate (2500) must fall within acceptable parameters, or the video will fail to play. You can use a conversion program on a desktop or laptop computer to convert video files such as your vacation movies shot with a DV camcorder to a format that will play on your Fire.

There is an excellent free, open source program for converting video files to the Fire format, and the program is available for the Windows PC, Apple Mac, and Ubuntu Linux machines. The program, Miro, can be downloaded at http://www.getmiro.com. The program may appear slightly complicated to use, at least initially. Fortunately, the getmiro.com website provides extensive documentation.

Importing your Music Library from other sources to your Fire

Import your iTunes, Microsoft Zune, or other music library into your Fire using the Amazon Cloud Player. Amazon has an easy to use tool that makes importing your iTunes of other music library a simple matter. Open a browser window on your computer, and visit http://www.amazon.com/cloudplayer (if you are in North America) or visit http://www.amazon.co.uk/cloudplayer (if you are in the United Kingdom) and set up a CloudPlayer account. Once you set up an account, click the Import Music button at the upper left, and follow the directions that appear on the screen. After you've imported your songs into the Amazon Cloud Player, you can select any number of songs, click the download button, and download them to your Fire.

Downloading and playing YouTube videos

Download YouTube videos for later playback on your Fire. YouTube has long supported the H.264 video encoding format that is currently used by the Fire. And if a subject has ever been recorded on video, chances are that it can be found on YouTube, at least in partial, if not in complete form. YouTube is known for being the resource for millions of video clips. You don't even have to resort to using a PC or a Mac to download YouTube videos, because numerous YouTube video downloader apps are available for the Fire. A search of the Amazon app store for the phrase 'youtube downloader' will reveal a number of entries. One that has been tested by this author is the Droid Youtube Downloader by KastorSoft. The app is simple to use, it does what is expected of it, and it is free. (The app is ad supported, but the ads are small and fairly unobtrusive.)

Install the app, and its operation is simplicity itself. You launch the app, and a search box appears at the top of the screen. Type a search term, tap the magnifying glass, and the app will search the entire YouTube database for videos that match your search term. Find a desired video and tap the video, and another menu appears. From this menu, you can choose to preview the video, download the file as video, download the file as an MP3 audio file, or download the file as an AAC video file. Select Download as Video, and you will see a message indicating the percentage of progress saved, then a message indicating when the download is complete.

Once the YouTube video has completed downloading, go to your Apps screen and bring up your Personal Videos app. You will see an icon displaying the starting screen of the YouTube video, and you can tap the icon to play the video.

Storing pictures and personal videos in the Amazon CloudDrive

Under the heading of 'Where's My Data?, chapter 1 introduced the concept of cloud based storage, which greatly increases your possible maximum storage space by saving data to web servers that reside on the Internet. As far as multimedia goes, you can store your photos and personal videos in the cloud, on Amazon's CloudDrive, to be specific. If you tap the Photos option on the Navigation bar and you never set up a CloudDrive account at Amazon, you'll see a welcome screen like the following:

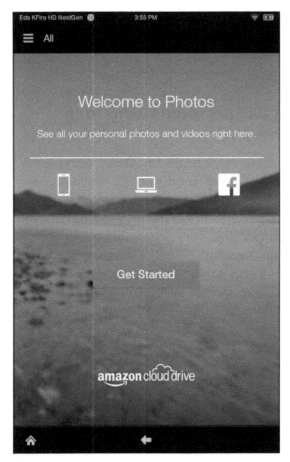

Click the Get Started link, and you will first be asked if you wish to send an app to your smartphone. (The app lets you view photos or videos stored in the Amazon cloud on your smartphone, or upload photos or videos from your phone to the Amazon cloud.) Confirm if you wish by clicking Yes and by entering your cell phone number where prompted.

Next, you will be asked if you want a link for the CloudDrive app sent to your PC. Click Yes if desired, and you will receive a link via e-mail that lets you download the Amazon CloudDrive app for your Windows or Apple IOS-based PC.

Once you've installed the app on a compatible smartphone or personal computer, you can move photos from your phone or your PC to Amazon's CloudDrive storage.

Viewing your CloudDrive photos on a Fire

After you've set up your CloudDrive account and uploaded any photos, just tap Photos in the Navigation bar on your Fire. Your photos will appear in a tiled based layout like that shown in the following illustration:

You can tap on any photo and it expands to fill your Fire's screen, like the example shown:

Press ⬆ symbol to move up to tiled view of all photos.

Tap Delete to remove photo.

Tap Share icon to share photo via e-mail, Facebook, or Twitter.

You can also perform a long press (press and hold) on any photo in your collection, and a popup menu will appear. Your menu choices are Share, Edit, Info, Download, and Delete.

Share lets you share the photo, either by means of an e-mail account, or through Facebook or Twitter, if these are linked to your Fire by means of the social settings.

Edit launches the native Kindle Photo Editor that you can use to make basic changes to your photos. You can change the brightness or contrast, crop your photo, reduce red eye, apply filters, and apply other special effects.

Info displays digital information stored about the photo, including the filename, creation date, dimensions (in pixels), and file size.

Download downloads the photo onto your device from the Amazon cloud, so that you will not need a Wi-Fi connection to display the photo.

Delete deletes the photo from your device.

The Amazon Cloud Storage account provides you with 5 GB of storage space, which is roughly enough to store over 2200 average photos. This amount of storage space would easily consume most of what is available on a Fire purchased with the standard 8 GB of memory. Since the Amazon CloudDrive account costs you nothing with a 5 GB allotment, it is well worth your taking the time to install and use the Amazon CloudDrive app.

Chapter 8: Camera Tips, Trips, and Traps

One of the many features found in the Fire tablet is the inclusion of two digital cameras. Included are both a front-facing VGA digital camera, and a rear facing 2 megapixel camera that supports 720 pixel high-definition video.

The cameras can be used to take pictures with the built-in Camera app, or with a number of 3rd-party applications available from the Amazon Appstore. You can use the cameras for video chat with the Skype app, available as a free download from the Amazon AppStore. You can also use the Facebook or Instagram apps to take and share photos with your social network friends.

When viewing the Fire with its volume buttons facing upwards, the front-facing camera is located within the small circle at the top center of the device, while the rear-facing camera can be found at the upper-left corner on the rear of the Fire tablet.

The front-facing camera is a VGA-resolution camera, and there is no flash on either camera, so don't expect great results under low lighting. The rear-facing camera is a 2.0 megapixel camera that supports high definition video at a 720-pixel setting. The rear camera performs well, and the front camera performs adequately under average lighting conditions. With the built-in camera app (as well as with most third-party camera apps), there are a number of user adjustable features that can enhance the quality of photos or videos. Since the front facing camera is facing towards you as you view the screen, it's clear that Amazon designed it initially to support video chatting or video conferencing with apps such as the Skype app. Since the initial release of the Fire tablets, the built-in Camera app has undergone a number of improvements that let you do much more with the built-in cameras than just video chat and take simple portraits, and that is the subject of this chapter.

Using the Fire's built-in Camera app

A basic camera app comes built into the Fire software, and it does a perfectly acceptable job of taking basic pictures or videos. Before taking any photos or videos with the camera, you should take the time to ensure that the camera lens is clean and free of any dust or other obstructions. Once you've done so, get to the Home screen, swipe up to display all of your Apps, and locate and tap the Camera icon to open the Camera app. The following illustration shows the screen and the controls that are visible when you use the Camera App.

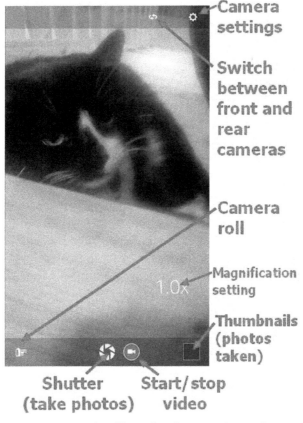

(Fire camera controls. Tap the image to enlarge.)

Tap the Shutter control to take photos in Camera mode, or tap the Start/Stop Video control to begin or end video recording.

With video recording, you can pinch the screen with two fingers to zoom in, or spread two fingers apart on the screen to zoom outwards. Once recording begins, tapping the Start/Stop Video control again will stop the video recording.

TIP ▶ **With the rear camera, use the Volume buttons as a zoom control.** The rear-facing camera has a Zoom feature that is activated through the use of the volume buttons on the Fire. By default, the camera starts at 1X magnification. Pressing the volume-up button increases the magnification to a maximum of 2X (twice normal size), and once increased, pressing the volume-down button decreases the magnification.

Viewing photos with the Camera Roll

After you've taken a photo or recorded a video, you can tap the thumbnail to see your most recent photos or videos. You can swipe to the left or to the right to move through the photos and videos contained in your Camera Roll.

To edit, delete, or view details (such as the creation date and time of your photos or videos), tap a desired photo within the Camera Roll and a window will open containing a small preview of the image, along with a menu of options at the left of the preview image, as shown in the following illustration.

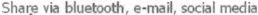
Share via bluetooth, e-mail, social media

The menu provides you with these options: Share, Delete, Edit, and Full-screen. Use the Share option to share the photo via a compatible Bluetooth device, to delete the photo, edit the photo, or change to a full-screen view of the photo.

Editing and Deleting Photos

Once you've taken photos with your Fire tablet, you can view, edit, and share those photos (as well as delete the ones you don't care for). Get to the Home screen and swipe upwards to show all of your apps, then tap Photos and swipe in from the left edge of the screen to display your photos. From this point, you can tap *Camera Roll* in order to view your recent photos or videos taken with either of the Fire tablet's built in cameras. You can also tap *All* to view all photos and videos that have been saved to the device or to the Amazon Cloud, and you can tap *Videos* to view just personal videos that are saved on your device or in the Amazon Cloud.

You can add photos or videos to your library for viewing on your Fire tablet. To do so, tap *Add Photos*, and from the menu that appears, tap *Mobile Device* (to import from Bluetooth-compatible devices), *PC or Mac*, *Facebook*, or *Transfer to USB*. You can then follow the instructions that appear on the screen to import your photos onto your Fire tablet.

When any single photo is visible on the Camera Roll, tapping **Edit** brings up a built-in photo editor which lets you apply a variety of effects to your photo, such as changing the brightness or contrast, modifying exposure levels and eliminating 'redeye,' cropping, and adding text or drawings to a photo. While viewing any photo, tap the photo to display the photo, and then tap the Edit icon to launch the Photo Editor. When the Photo Editor starts, you will see a menu at the bottom of the screen that displays a variety of photo editing categories, as shown in the following illustration.

Tap any category to view the editing tools for that category. If there is just one tool in a category, you will be taken to that tool. If there are multiple tools for a category, simply tap a desired tool to use it.

When you are finished editing the photo, tap *Apply* to save your edits. (If you decide not to use a chosen photo editing tool, swipe up from the bottom of the screen to return to the Photo Editor categories.)

When you are finished using the Photo Editor, tap *Done* at the upper right to exit from the app.

Sharing your photos with others

While you are displaying any photo or video in the Camera Roll, you can tap the Share icon in the toolbar area, to bring up a menu of sharing options that you can use to share photos or videos with friends. The Share icon is shown here:

Tap the icon, and a menu of choices that include Twitter, Facebook, Bluetooth devices, and e-mail appears. (Additional choices may appear on this menu, depending on the apps that you have installed on your device.) You can select any of those choices to share your photos or videos by means of the Twitter or Facebook social networks, by means of an e-mail attachment, or by means of another app on your device that has photo-sharing capabilities, such as Pinterest or Instagram.

An important note about photo & video storage and the Amazon Cloud Drive

By default, all photos and videos that you take using the built-in cameras of any Kindle Fire are backed up to your Amazon Cloud Drive account. If you do not want this copying of your files to the Amazon Cloud Drive to occur, drag the menu outwards from the left edge of the screen, tap Settings, and then turn the **Automatic Updates** option to **Off**.

Getting photos from your Fire onto your computer

TIP You can copy photos from your Fire directly to your computer. One way to move photos from your Fire to your computer is to send the photos by e-mail, but there's another method that is often faster, especially when you have a large number of photos. You can transfer photos from your Fire to your computer using the following steps. First, connect the Fire to the computer using the USB cable. Open the Computer folder on your computer. (If you are running Windows, you can go to the Start menu and select Computer.) Open the Computer folder and select Fire, then open that folder and select the Internal Storage folder. Open the Internal Storage folder and look for a folder named DCIM.

Open the DCIM folder and look for a folder named Camera. Open the Camera folder, and you will see your photos taken with the camera. Select the photos that you want to transfer to your computer, then right click and select Cut from the menu that appears if you want to move the photos from your Fire, or select Copy from the menu that appears if you want to keep a copy of the photos on your Fire. Finally, navigate to the folder on your computer where you want to place your photos, then right click and select Paste.

NOTE: **If you can't find your photos, try a reset.** At times, the Fire's MediaScanner service does not see new pictures immediately. In order for photos and videos to show up, they have to be scanned and indexed by the MediaScanner service that is a part of the operating system running on the Fire. If you wait long enough, they will eventually show up, but you can force them to appear by simply restarting your Fire.

TIP You can quickly delete unwanted photos while viewing them. When any photo is visible, perform a long-press near the center of the photo. When a popup menu appears, tap "Delete" to delete the photo.

Adding capabilities with third-party camera apps

If you plan to make any extensive use of the Fire's built in cameras, you may want to download a camera app for your machine. While the built-in camera app provides a variety of editing capabilities, a number of third-party camera apps provide additional capabilities, such as increased zoom, special effects, delay timers, and the ability to pause and resume video recordings. A search of the Amazon AppStore for the phrase 'camera app' will reveal an assortment of dozens of apps. (When shopping for a camera app—or for any 3rd-party app for that matter—examining the customer reviews is a wise idea, as the quality of 3rd-party apps in general ranges from outstanding to mediocre at best.)

General Camera tips

WARNING: <u>If you make use of an optional camera app purchased from the AppStore and your camera app has a 1080 pixel setting, do NOT try to use it with either camera on your Fire tablet!</u> Many third-party camera apps have a 1080 pixel setting within their video settings. This setting exists because these apps are written to run on other Android devices, many of which are based on hardware supporting the 1080 pixel resolution (such as the Fire HD8 or Fire HD10). The standard cameras on a Fire tablet do *not* support this resolution, and if you select such an option, the app will probably crash and you may have to restart your Fire. If the app that you are using has an option for resolution settings, avoid any settings higher than 720 pixels.

TIP **When filming video, you may need to turn the camera "upside down."** If you are using an optional third-party camera app that supports video filming, you may discover that the Fire gives proper results when the built-in camera is facing downwards, and not at the top of the device. (This behavior doesn't appear to affect all apps that support video, but it does appear to affect some third-party apps, so you may want to check the operation of your chosen app before attempting to record that all-important wedding or graduation using your Fire.)

Chapter 9: Apps Tips, Tricks, and Traps

In this chapter, we look at the power of apps to add significant features and capabilities to your Fire. The tablet would be impressive if it were only used for reading books and magazines, for watching movies and TV shows, and for web browsing. But with a range of apps available from the Amazon AppStore, you can transform your Fire in an unlimited number of ways. Using apps, you can literally transform your Fire into a news or weather information center, a sports scoreboard, an international language translator, a customized radio station, a medical adviser, or a personal butler that reminds you of every appointment on your busy daily schedule. And of course, you can use an app to make your Fire into a game platform, so that you can play a few rounds of Angry Birds. This chapter will first detail various tips, tricks, and traps for apps in general, in a section we like to call 'Apps 101.' We will follow that with a listing of twelve apps that we feel that no Fire should be without.

About Apps

Apps for your Fire (or for any tablet computer, for that matter) are actually computer programs, engineered to handle a specific task. As such, they must be ***installed*** on your Fire, which is a sophisticated computer in its own right. You install apps on your Fire by first purchasing the app (even if it's free) from the Amazon AppStore. Swipe the menu bar left or right and tap Apps to get to the Amazon Appstore. Next, tap the magnifying glass and enter a search term for the desired app (or browse among the popular apps displayed and select a desired app.

Once you are at the Appstore page for the desired app, tap the 'Buy' button to purchase or get the app. You can then install the app on your Fire by pressing the 'Download' button that appears. After the app has been downloaded to your Fire, the download button changes to display the word 'Open', and you can press the Open button to start the app. Once the app exists on your Fire, you can get to it at any time, by choosing Apps from the Home screen, and locating and pressing on the icon for the particular app.

Find and install the app you want. At the Home screen, tap Apps, then at the upper right, tap Store. When the main screen of the Amazon AppStore appears, tap in the Search AppStore box at the top of the screen. The box will expand, and the keyboard will appear within the lower portion of the screen. Enter a search term to bring up one or more apps matching your search term, then tap the icon for the app that you are looking for.

Can I run generic android apps that don't come from the Amazon AppStore?

The short answer to the above question is an unqualified "maybe," but it's also a topic that is far beyond the scope of this book. You may be aware of the fact that your Fire runs a modified version of the popular Android operating system originally developed by Google. And you may be aware of the existence of android apps from other sources on the web (such as Google's own Play Store). While it is possible to run some of these apps on a Fire, it takes some tinkering with settings, and it's not a practice that Amazon recommends. Nevertheless, if you are interested in pursuing this topic further, you are definitely moving into "geek" territory. As an accomplished geek, my recommendation is that (1) you tread very carefully when journeying into this area and (2) you refer to a "geek" level treatment of the topic. I've written a rather geeky book on the subject named *Sideloading your Fire*, and you can learn more about my book by clicking the following image.

Look inside ↓

Holiday Season 2014

Sideloading your Fire

Sideload Android apps, music, and video onto Fire devices

#1 best-selling AUTHOR

Edward Jones

kindle edition

Alternately, you can perform a Google search on the phrase, 'how to install playstore on the Fire,' and a number of articles will appear in response to the search. Some will be well-written, and others will make you regret having ever asked the question to begin with.

Deleting Apps

There will be times you'll want to delete an app, perhaps because it's not what you expected, or it is a game you've outgrown, or something better comes along. Apps are stored in two places: in your cloud storage on Amazon's servers, and on your Fire itself. When you initially purchase an app (even free apps are purchased, you just aren't charged for these), the app is stored in your personal space in the Amazon Cloud, where the app is not taking up any space on your Fire. When you press the download button that appears on the apps' icon in the cloud, it gets downloaded to the memory space of your Fire itself.

Remove unwanted apps from your Fire. You can remove any app from the Fire by performing a "long

109

press" on the apps icon, and choosing 'Remove from Device' from the popup menu that appears. The long press simply means that you press and hold your finger on the icon for a few seconds. At the Home screen, press Apps to display your apps screen. When the apps screen appears, select 'Device' near the top center of the screen, to display all the apps currently stored on your Fire.

Press and hold your finger on the icon of the unwanted app until a menu appears, then select 'Remove from Device' from the menu. This action will delete the app from your Kindle's memory space.

An app that's deleted from your Fire can still be taking up space in your cloud. Keep in mind that deleting an app from your Fire itself does not remove the app from your storage in the Amazon Cloud. If you want to delete the app from cloud storage as well, go to your Home screen, tap Apps, locate the unwanted app, press and hold your finger on the app icon until a popup menu appears, then choose 'Remove from Cloud' from the menu. *Note that deleting an app from your cloud storage at Amazon also wipes away any subscription information you may have saved in the app, so you should do this only if you are certain that you do not want to use the app in the future.*

Troubleshooting Apps

As mentioned earlier, apps are computer programs. And like all computer programs, they will at times fail to operate as promised, misbehave, or go absolutely haywire. When an app fails to operate as expected, your steps in resolving the issue will vary greatly depending on what type of behavior the app exhibited in the first place. Some app failures fall into the 'hiccup' category, in which case it may be best to chalk it up to the "evil gods of operating systems" and to move on in life. Other failures can go beyond the level of major annoyance; as an example, a camera app for my Fire recently caused my Fire's sound to stop working in all applications, and the only fix was to perform a hard reboot and completely reset my Fire to factory settings. If an app misbehaves, crashes, or completely locks up your Fire, here are some procedures that you can try, ranging in ascending order from minor (meaning, 'let's hope this works') to major (meaning, 'lets hope you don't have to resort to this')-

1. ***Close and restart the app.*** Without subjecting you to a heavy dose of techno-babble, let's just say that Android-based computers tend to be more stable than some small computer operating systems (Windows, not that anyone is pointing fingers) because each Android app runs in something called ***protected space.*** From a programming point of view, each app can "play inside its own sandbox." This means that in theory, the abnormal operation of an app should not affect the entire operating system, nor should it have an effect on other apps. When an app misbehaves, the least troublesome step is to completely close the app, then restart the app. If this does not fix the problem you can move on to-

2. ***Perform a soft reset on your Fire.*** This happens naturally whenever you power down the machine, so just try turning it off. Wait 10 seconds, and power the Fire back on, then try the app again. If the soft reset fails to bring your machine back to normal operation, you can resort to-

3. ***Perform a hard reset.*** With the Kindle powered up, press and hold the power button depressed until you see a "Shutdown Your Kindle?" prompt appear on the screen. Tap 'Yes' in response to this prompt, and your Kindle will shut down. Wait 10 seconds, and power your Kindle back up. You may notice a distinct difference in the appearance of the startup sequence this time, as the Amazon lettering "Fire" in white and orange will appear in the center of the screen, and will remain there for a short period of time (less than 2 minutes) while the machine restarts. Hopefully, this will fix

the issue, because the most drastic step will also result in a definite loss of settings. But if you must resort to the most drastic step--

4. ***Reset your Fire to its default directory settings***. Be warned that if use this last resort, you will need to reset your username and e-mail account information that you've registered with Amazon into the device, and you will have to pull all your apps back down from the Amazon cloud (and reenter any user settings that may have been stored in these apps). To perform this ultimate reboot, use the following steps:

a. At the Home screen, tap and drag down from the top of the screen, and tap Settings.

b. At the next screen, choose 'Device.'

c. At the next screen, choose 'Restore your device to Factory Settings.'

If your Fire still has operational issues after this type of reset, it is definitely time to get on the phone with Amazon Customer Service.

Twelve FREE Apps That No Fire Should Be Without

As promised, here's a listing of 12 FREE apps (you heard correctly, the price is zero, nada, zilch) that this author believes should be on the carousel of every Fire. This is an admittedly subjective list, but each of these apps has also received a high average rating (between 4 and 5 stars) from Amazon reviewers (with the exception of Facebook, which received three stars but is nevertheless included due to the massive popularity of Facebook). We've also taken the time to include links back to the Amazon order pages for each of these apps. So if any of these apps suits your fancy, just click the title or the app's icon, and you will be taken to the Amazon page for that app, where you can click the 'Get App' button to download the app to your Fire.

Note that the write-ups of the free apps that follow are excerpted from the publication, *Top 300 (Plus) Free Apps for the Kindle Fire* by this same author. If you would like to see the remaining recommendations detailed in that book, consider clicking this link and spending the reasonable sum of ninety-nine cents on *Top 300 (Plus) Free Apps for the Kindle Fire* by Edward Jones.

Crackle

Crackle is an outstanding source of FREE (that's correct, as in 'no subscrber or pay-per-view fees imvolved) movies and TV shows. With the Crackle app installed on yor Kindle Fire, you get immediate access to thousands of full-length Hollywood movies and TV shows. At the time this was written, the lineup on Crackle included movies like Pineapple Express, Big Daddy, Joe Dirt, Mr. Deeds, Alien Hunter, The Deep, Panic Room, S.W.A.T., and hundreds of others. Also in the Crackle lineup are dozens of TV shows like Seinfeld, The Prisoner, Marvel Comics' Iron Man animated series, All in the Family, and Chosen, just to name a few. Twenty new movies and TV episodes are added to the lineup each month, from genres that include action, anime, comedy, crime, horror, thrillers, and sci-fi. Crackle is truly free internet entertainment at its best, and unless you only purchased your Fire for reading, you shuld definitely have the Crackle app as one of your apps.

Netflix

The app may be free, but of course you'll need a Netflix subscription to actually watch any content. Given that fact, if you are a Netflix subscriber, you'll want the free Netflix app for your Fire. You can watch all of the same Netflix videos that you might see streamed to your laptop, and if you've got a Fire, you can enjoy that Dolby surround sound which comes across nicely with a good pair of headphones plugged into the Kindle. Log in with your NetFlix account, and you can get their usual unlimited shows and flicks on your Fire, and can even pick up where you left off on a show you'd started watching earlier on your TV set or other portable device. Of course, no movie-viewing app would be complete without having the Internet Movie Database (IMDb) app so you can get a good idea of what you're watching before you decide to watch it; the Internet Movie Database app is described next.

IMDb

      If you are a movie fan or a fan of regular TV shows, or even if you aren't but don't want to be embarrassed by those trivia-type TV actor questions that arise when you and your friends are debating "who played in what role," you'll want IMDb on your Fire. The app gives you access to a database of two million titles and four million cast members. It is divided into movies and TV sections, you can see what U.S. movies are getting the highest box office ratings, and you can even watch trailers for hundreds of thousands of movies. The app doesn't have anything that you couldn't get from the IMDb web site running on your laptop for desktop computer, but the interface is intuitive, the app is free, and it's easy to carry around on your Fire.

USA Today

      From what multiple reviewers and this author say, the USA Today app for the Kindle Fire is the kind of app that every newspaper app should be. The content is beautiful, optimized to take advantage of the Fire's larger screen. Unlike many newspaper apps for Android-based tablets, the content is all free on this one; there are no subscription services to pay whatsoever. While you're online, the app feeds you constant updates, making sure you've received the latest news and information, and you can pull down stories for offline reading when you don't have Internet access.

      The organization is logical, the formatting is colorful, and from a user friendliness standpoint it's a cinch to navigate. There is a wonderfully-intuitive 'swipe to the left or right' action within the main content viewer that automatically jumps you between stories in the smaller Articles window on the left, or you can tap any story within the Articles window to bring up the corresponding story on the right. Stories are laced with vivid video narratives. As an online newspaper, this implementation absolutely rocks. Oh, and did we mention that it's free? As a newspaper, USA Today on the Fire deserves five stars.

The Weather Channel

For the kind of in-depth weather reporting that you've come to rely on, you no longer need to turn to a cable or satellite TV channel. The Weather Channel is now no further than your Fire. Get animated and customizable radar maps; immediate, 36-hour, and ten day forecasts; severe weather alerts for the US and Europe; the ability to save multiple locations; and a "find me" feature that provides you with pinpoint local weather, based on your GPS location. Even the local pollen counts, which are often omitted from other sources, can be found at The Weather Channel. One particularly nice feature is the ability to touch a 'Video' button and get the local forecast for your area on demand from one of the TV anchors for The Weather Channel.

ESPN ScoreCenter

     When it comes time to talk sports around the office water cooler on a Monday morning, you'll never be stumped for a score again if you install the ESPN ScoreCenter app on your Fire. You'll get scores, team standings, and news from hundreds of sports leagues worldwide. The variety of sports provided by ESPN ScoreCenter is just short of breathtaking-you'll find NFL and college football, NBA and college basketball, Major League Baseball, NHL Ice Hockey, and most other NCAA sports. If you are a big soccer fan, you'll find coverage of the Premier League, UEFA Champions League, the World Cup, and hundreds of additional soccer leagues and tournaments. NASCAR and Indy racing fans will find full coverage of motor sports, and golf, tennis, rugby, and cricket fans are all covered as well. If you are looking to keep up with the sports scene, you'll find it all in the ESPN ScoreCenter app.

Facebook by Facebook

This is the Facebook app for the Fire, engineered by the programmers at Facebook. It's basically the same app that was created by Facebook for generic Android-based tablets, with a few tweaks in the programming code to allow it to run under the heavily modified version of the Android operating system used by the Fire.

If you are familiar with Facebook, you have an idea of what to expect, and you do get these basics from the Facebook app. The news feed is here, and a new button at the upper right of the news feed quickly shows you who among your Facebook friends is available to message. When sending messages from within the app, you can see who is active, so you will have an idea as to when you can expect a reply. As with Facebook from the web, you can see what your friends are up to; share updates, photos, and videos; get notifications when others 'like' or comment on your posts; and text, chat, and carry on group conversations.

All that being said, the Facebook app gets a 'middle of the road' rating from Amazon reviewers, having had its fair share of teething problems. The most commonly experienced problem, according to numerous Amazon reviewers, is an inability to see more than roughly ten posts in your message wall or in the news feed. This problem has been reported to Facebook for about as long as the Facebook app has been in existence (which has been for some months now). If you install a Facebook app and you encounter the same type of behavior, you may want to uninstall the app and consider other ways to get to Facebook, one of which is mentioned in the paragraphs that follow.

Calculator Plus FREE by Digital Cherry, LLC

This app earned a listing in a "best free apps" article written by USA Today, and for good reason. Calculator Plus consistently earns five stars from reviewers, thanks to its intuitive interface, its feature set, and its ease of use. It is a simple calculator with just the basics, but those basics likely make for 98% of what most people need in a calculator. The app takes advantage of the Fire's large screen to present a very basic, but totally functional desktop style calculator. You get the basic keys (+), (-), (*), (/), and (%), along with a backspace key that works intuitively in concert with the calculator's multiline display, allowing you to use the backspace key to "undo" past operations. This free app is ad supported, but the ads are unobtrusive and nearly impossible to accidentally hit while using the calculator function keys.

Kayak

by Kayak Software Corporation

Kayak is a great multipurpose travel app for your Fire that lets you search for and discover flights, hotels, and car rentals, compare prices, and even get notification of cancellations and delays and gate information for your flights. You can also access maps of restaurants and ATMs in different locations where you are travelling. If you're in need of a last minute hotel room, or worried about a gate change or a flight delayed due to weather conditions, or need a car rental or you would just like to see a map of the airport where you're making a connection, you can now do all of this in one single app, Kayak. One caveat is that the app appears to only use Hertz as a car rental source, but otherwise, this is a great app for all things travel related.

CruiseFinder

by iCruise.com

If you are a fan of cruising, this is one app that you'll want to have on your Fire. Cruise Finder is a comprehensive cruise vacation planning app that gives you extensive information concerning over 200 ships sailing with 20 different cruise lines. You'll find thousands of itineraries complete with day by day descriptions and route maps, online pricing, availability, and booking, photos of ports, stateroom descriptions and deck plans, and even parking and map information for cruise line ports. A 'Hot Cruise Deals' section keeps you up to date with last minute pricing, and a 'My Favorites' section lets you save your favorite ships, itineraries, and cruise lines.

YP Local Search and Gas Prices (Kindle tablet edition)

by YP

When your travel is more of the local variety, out and around your own hometown, the people behind the yellow pages have brought you a great little free app called YP Local Search and Gas Prices. You can search through over 16,000,000 businesses divided into major categories like restaurants, bars, hotels, doctors, dentists, mechanics, and more. You can check out the menus from over 300,000 restaurants, and you can find the gas stations that have the best gas prices in town. You can personalize your version of the app so that it is gives you fast access to nearby businesses, restaurants, and events in your town, and you can provide your own feedback by rating local businesses (you'll need to be online to enter ratings). If you live in an area of the country where gas prices can vary wildly from one neighborhood to another, this app can be worth having just for the possible savings in gas prices alone.

iTranslate by Sonico Mobile

iTranslate is a great free app that does language translation. If you're a student of languages or you do a lot of international travel, you'll definitely want to have this one on your Fire. The app does a magnificent job of combining voice recognition with voice output, so you can speak and see your language. The app will translate words, phrases, and entire sentences into any one of more than 50 languages. These words of one Amazon reviewer do a great job of describing the functionality of the program:

"I am fluent in several languages and was pretty impressed with this app. I tested with a realistic tourist phrase which was fairly complex "I would like to visit your best art museum. Can you give me a recommendation and how to get there."

I selected English from the left drop down list, typed in the phrase in English, and selected the second language from a drop down list on the right. I was impressed with the translation, the grammar was perfectly correct. Next to the text there was a button which pronounced the translation. The pronunciation was excellent and sounded like a native speaker. The intonations sounded "computer generated" but completely understandable. I tested Russian and Spanish." The reviewer goes on to state that "this was the first random sentence that came to mind, I did not try to find a phrase that would be translated well. I was quite impressed with the results."

iTranslate will even let you e-mail a translated message, share it via Twitter, or copy it into memory for use with another app. Supported languages (at the time of this writing) include the following: Afrikaans, Albanian, Arabic, Belarusian, Bulgarian, Catalan, Chinese Simplified, Chinese Traditional, Croatian, Czech, Danish, Dutch, English, Estonian, Finnish, French, Galician, German, Greek, Hebrew, Hindi, Hungarian, Icelandic, Indonesian, Italian, Irish, Japanese, Korean, Latvian, Lithuanian, Macedonian, Malay, Maltese, Norwegian, Persian, Polish, Portuguese, Romanian, Russian, Serbian, Slovak, Slovenian, Spanish, Swahili, Swedish, Tagalog, Thai, Turkish, Ukrainian, Vietnamese, Welsh, and Yiddish.

As mentioned earlier, the write-ups of the 12 free apps described in this chapter were excerpted from the publication, Top 300 (Plus) Free Apps for the Kindle Fire by this same author. If you would like to see the other recommendations detailed in that book, consider searching the Amazon website for the following title and spending the reasonable sum of ninety-nine cents on *Top 300 (Plus) Free Apps for the Kindle Fire by Edward Jones.*

Chapter 10: Printing from your Fire

If your printer supports wireless printing, you can print documents, emails, photos, webpages, and calendar events directly from your Fire tablet. Modern printers that support wireless printing will appear in a list of printers when you print from within a printer-compatible app or document on your Fire tablet. If your printer does not appear in the list of printers displayed on your fire, you may need to install a print plug-in from the Amazon Appstore. You can find the names of compatible printers on each of the following product pages of the Amazon Appstore:

Epson: www.amazon.com/dp/B00ENB2CSK
HP: www.amazon.com/dp/B00EDUTGB2
Canon: www.amazon.com/dp/B00E19FB28
Samsung:
www.amazon.com/dp/B00DMZ3AM0
Ricoh: www.amazon.com/dp/B00FAX29AG

To print from your tablet, first ensure that your printer is turned on and is connected via Wi-Fi to the same network that is providing a Wi-Fi signal to your Fire tablet. You can then perform these steps to print:

1. Open the document, webpage, email, or other item that you wish to print.

2. Tap the menu icon (the three vertical dots) and when the menu opens, tap Print.

3. Select your printer from the list of printers that appears. (If your printer does not appear in the list, tap All Printers to search for printers on your network, or tap the + symbol to add a printer using the IP address of the printer. If you don't know your printer's IP address, refer to the documentation packaged with your printer for assistance.)

4. Select the number of copies you wish to print.

5. Tap More Options if you wish to make any changes to the color mode, paper size, or orientation.

6. Tap Print.

TIP if you don't have Internet access, you can save Microsoft Office documents and web pages as PDF files, and print these files at a later time when you have Internet access within reach of a wireless printer. Save a file as a PDF file, tap the menu icon (the three vertical dots) for the document or web page that you want to save and then tap Print. Choose Save as PDF and then tap the PDF icon. Later, when you have Internet access and you need to print the PDF file, at the Home screen swipe in the menu bar and tap Local storage, then tap documents and use the menu icon (described above) to print the document.

Printing using Google's Cloud Print Services

With all that a Fire can do (and if you've used various apps, you probably already noticed that it can do a lot), there's one shortcoming. Natively, there's no direct support for wired printing. You cannot just connect your Fire to a printer using a USB cable and print documents, emails, web pages, or other content. But with the right combination of apps and free services, you can print directly from your Fire to print to printers that may not be on the above list of printers. You can use Google Cloud Print, a free service that is linked to a Google account, to print to compatible printers. Once you set up Google Cloud Print to work with a printer, you'll need an app like EasyPrint. Search the Amazon website for 'easy print app' to locate the download page for this app.

First, get a Google account if you don't already have one, and set up Google Cloud Print using your Google account. You can find full instructions explaining how to do this at http://www.google.com/cloudprint. Google Cloud Print is a web-based technology that lets you print to wi-fi enabled printers via the internet. You can print to printers that are "cloud-ready," or printers that can connect directly to the internet without a connection to a computer. Using Google Cloud Print, you can also connect to older (so-called "classic") printers if they are connected to a Windows, Mac, or Linux computer with Internet access, and Google's Chrome web browser is installed and running on the computer.

Once you've set up your wi-fi equipped printer to work with Google Cloud Print, go to the Home screen of your Fire, tap Apps, tap Store, and search for EasyPrint. The app is free (it's advertiser supported, but the ads are sufficiently unobtrusive). After you download and install the app, you will need to tell EasyPrint your Google account username and password, and you will need to specify a default printer that all print jobs should be sent to. You can then use the menu bar options within EasyPrint to choose what is to be printed from your Fire. (The following illustration shows the EasyPrint app running on the author's Fire.)

EasyPrint

Default:
<none>

Google accounts

Printers

Print jobs

Print document

Print Google Docs

Print from storage

You can choose documents stored on your Fire, pdf files, web pages, or documents stored on Google Drive under your Google account. As the illustration shows, you can also choose your Google accounts to be used with EasyPrint (you can have more than one Google account used by the app), you can view all print jobs sent to your printer using Google Cloud Print, and you can view the status of your cloud-based printers (if you have more than one printer registered with Google Cloud Print).

There are other apps available that will also let you print on your Fire using Google Cloud Print. Two that are free and work well are printer model specific; they are the Kodak Document Print App (works with Kodak printers), and the Hewlett Packard ePrint App (works with HP printers). If you happen to own a Kodak printer that is cloud ready, one nice feature of the Kodak app is that it also lets you assign an e-mail address (such as 'myprinter@kodakeprint.com') to your printer. Once you assign this address, you can send emails with or without attachments to the address from any device, not just from your Fire, and the e-mail plus any attachments will be printed on your Kodak printer.

If you've enabled two-step verification for added security on your Google account, you are likely to have issues getting EasyPrint or any of the Google Cloud

Print-compatible apps to operate successfully on your Fire. This doesn't appear to be a limitation of the Fire; as of this writing, the author has been unable to use a Google account that has two-step verification enabled to operate with cloud printing from *any* device, including Google's own Nexus tablet. Your recommended option in this case is to set up a separate Google account, do not enable two-step verification on that account, and use the account solely for cloud printing.

Chapter 11: Security Tips, Tricks, and Traps

Amazon has managed to marry what is basically an Android-based tablet computer with the near-flawless customer service experience that makes for shopping with the company, and the result-- the Fire-- makes for a consumer experience that, in terms of ease of use, is hard to beat. That same design advantage, in the wrong hands, could be a major security risk. For that reason, this chapter provides some tips on securing your Fire.

Lock your Fire. An unlocked Fire is somewhat akin to an unlocked car with the keys left in the ignition. If you lose your Fire, or the device is stolen, whoever happens to "acquire" it could read your email, access your Facebook account, and possibly order a number of expensive items from Amazon by mail before you became aware of the loss. Make sure your Fire requires a login password to prevent unauthorized users from gaining access to the machine's content. At the Home screen, swipe down from the top of the screen, and tap Settings at the upper-right to display the Settings options. Tap Security, then turn on "Lock Screen Password." Enter a password, then enter it a second time to confirm.

Make a note of your password in a secure location, if you are the type that forgets passwords. If you do lock down your Fire and you forget the password, the only way to restore operation of the device is to perform a default factory reset, which will also erase all of your existing settings and take the machine back to the factory "out of the box" condition.

Back up your machine's settings to the Amazon Cloud on a regular basis. You can easily backup your device settings simply by using the Sync feature on the Settings screen. Every so often (perhaps monthly), swipe down from the top of the screen, tap Settings, scroll upwards, and under the 'System' category, tap **Sync Device**. Doing so will not only synchronize things such as your email and contacts, but also the general settings for the device will be backed up to your account in the Amazon Cloud. This way, if the device ever needs replacing, you will save a significant amount of time as you will be able to pull your settings from the Amazon Cloud down into the replacement device.

Restrict purchasing and browsing with Parental Controls. If you have young ones around the house that also use your Fire, may want to turn on parental controls to prevent young ones from surfing the web's more inappropriate locations, and to prevent their making unauthorized purchases as well. At the Home screen, swipe down from the top of the screen, tap Settings at the upper-right, and then tap Parental Controls. Change the option to ON, and enter a password twice to activate parental controls.

Check out the Amazon Help Video.

Amazon has taken the time to provide a short help video explaining household profiles which can be used to create child profiles that you then use to implement parental controls. At the Amazon web site, tap or click

'Help' (just below the Search box), and at the next page, under 'Browse Help Topics' select 'Amazon devices' and at the right, choose 'Fire HD8' or 'Fire HD10' as is appropriate. Under 'Settings and Security,' tap or click 'Share your device with household profiles on Fire tablet.'

Tip or Trap, you decide: **Restrict applications to Amazon apps**. By default, the Fire is set to only permit apps from the Amazon AppStore to be installed. There is an option under device settings to allow installation of apps from unknown sources. There are pros and cons to either choice, which is why I've listed this as a tip or a trap. On my Fire, I allow apps from other sources to be installed, but I'm an admitted geek. If you don't know what you are doing, or if you are not fully aware of the source of the apps that you download, you may want to leave this option turned off and stick with the Amazon AppStore for all your applications. (To change this option, swipe down from the top of the screen and tap Settings at the upper-right, then under 'Personal' tap Security, and change the 'Apps from External Sources' to Yes or No, depending on your preference.)

Chapter 12: Battery and Power Tips, Tricks, and Traps

One of the many strong points of the Fire is its battery life. The Fire tablet is rated in excess of 7 hours between charges, and that's quite an engineering accomplishment given the Fire's bright, high definition screen. But for those times when you may spend hours and hours away from an electrical outlet, there are specific tips that can help you get more out of your Fire's battery life and go for longer periods of time between charges.

Dim the screen, lengthen the battery life. Much of the power consumed by your Fire goes toward lighting that high definition screen, and the brighter the screen is lit, the more power that gets consumed. So when you're seated in that cramped tin can called an airliner at 30,000 feet, flying across the Pacific, turn down the brightness. Swipe down from the top of the screen and tap Settings at the upper-right, to open the Settings screen. Tap Display, and move the slider for Display Brightness down to a level that's comfortable for reading. (Your battery will last longer, and you can always turn the brightness back up after you're at the hotel in Honolulu!)

Adjust your screen timeout. By default, your Fire automatically dims its screen after a certain period of inactivity. You can adjust the time period, and the shorter the period, the longer your battery life. Swipe down from the top of the screen and tap Settings at the upper-right, to open the Settings screen. Tap Display then tap Display Sleep, and set this to as short a time as you are comfortable with.

tip! Shut down wi-fi when there's no chance of getting a wi-fi signal. In places where there is no chance of getting a working wi-fi signal (such as most commuter rail lines and most aircraft), the wireless circuitry inside your Fire doesn't know any better and stays unusually active, checking for a wi-fi signal and consuming an abnormally high amount of battery power. An easy way to prevent this is to switch to airplane mode, which disables the Fire's wi-fi. (You will still be able to access any content you've already downloaded, such as your books, music, most apps, Amazon videos downnloaded for offline viewing, and any personal videos that are stored on your device.) Drag down from the top of the screen, and in the Quick Settings window, turn on Airplane Mode. (When you are back in range of a strong wi-fi signal, remember to turn off Airplane Mode).

tip! Use earphones in place of the built in speaker. Most headphones and earphones use much less power than the built-in speaker of the Fire.

tip! Every so often, run down the battery on purpose. If you're the type of individual that keeps your rechargeable devices connected to a wall outlet, you may actually be shortening your battery life in the long run. The type of battery used by the Fire (as is used by other tablets and most laptop computers) actually loses its effectiveness over time if it is constantly kept in a state of near-full charge. The way to prevent this is to perform what is called a "deep discharge"—you intentionally allow your battery to run down closer to the point of exhaustion before recharging your device. Doing this on a monthly basis will help keep your Fire's battery working near top-notch condition.

CONCLUSION (and a favor to ask!)

I truly hope that you enjoy using your Fire tablet as much as I have enjoyed using mine and writing about the Fire. As an author, I'd love to ask a favor: if you have the time, please consider writing a short review of this book. Honest reviews help me to write better books. At the Amazon website, tap or click the 'My Orders tab, find your order for this publication, and tap or click the 'Write a review' button. And my sincere thanks for your time!

I do feel that Amazon's Fire is one awesome tablet, and as a technology writer I've got plenty to compare it to (in my household, we have a number of Fire tablets and Kindle e-readers, Samsung and Google Nexus tablets, and an Apple iPad). So many people think the Fire tablet product line is just for reading books and watching movies, but machines like the Fire can do so much more. Hopefully, after you have had the opportunity to try some of the many tips and tricks that have been outlined in this guide, you'll discover that for yourself.

-Ed Jones

Join our mailing list...

We would be honored to add your name to our mailing list, where we can keep you informed of any book updates and of additional tips or topics about the Fire. Our mailing list will NEVER be sold to others (because we hate spam as much as you probably do), and the only information that we will ask you to supply is a valid e-mail address. To join our mailing list, go to www.thekindlewizard.com and click the "join mailing list" option within the menu.

Other books by the author:

Top 300 Free Apps for the Fire is your guide to 300 of the top rated apps that you'll find useful for your Fire. Jones has taken the time to research and compile this extensive list of apps for your Fire, and best of all, each of these apps are FREE. You'll find apps for the home office, for entertainment, for news, weather, and sports, for your health, for managing your finances, for playing games, and more. A local news apps section provides news, weather, and traffic apps for over 50 major US cities, and a travel section gives you an insight to the best apps that will help you find great deals on flights, hotel rooms, cruises, dining, and even the best gas prices around your hometown or when on the road. Each listing begins with a clickable link back to the Amazon catalog. So as you read this book on your Kindle, if any particular app sounds like what you've been looking for, just tap the image or heading name. You'll be taken directly to the Amazon page for the app, where you can click the button to install that app. (Active wi-fi connection required.) Let Top 300 Free Apps for the Fire be your guide to the best free apps for your new tablet!

To visit the author's Amazon page for a complete list of books, click the link below and then click the Kindle Books link:

http://www.amazon.com/author/edwardjones_writer

All-New Fire Tablet Tips, Tricks, and Traps: A guide to the new under $50 fire tablet

by Edward Jones

.